ENOUGH.

God and the Fine Art of Measuring Up

Dave Weiss

Enough

Published Mohrsville, Pennsylvania, by David C. Weiss for AMOK-Books, a division of AMOKArts.com, AMOKArts.com is a trademark of David C. Weiss

Illustrations by David C. Weiss

ISBN-13: 978-1979934114
ISBN-10: 1979934118

Library of Congress Cataloging-in Publication Data
Weiss, David C,. 1963-

Enough. Using God's Word to Answer the Age Old
Question—Am I Enough?

1. Weiss, David C., 1963- 2. religion 3. Spirituality 4. Christian Living

Contents

Enough

Enough.

To my wife Dawn, who showed me how to be enough and my sons Brandon and Chris, I hope I've showed you that you're enough.

Foreword

I was high when I got the idea for this book...

Okay, I better qualify that because I am hoping my friends and family, not to mention the many people who call me "pastor" and those who come to hear me speak, will read it. The kind of high I was having was the kind of high I wish for my children, grandchildren, and pretty much everyone else I love, to experience and experience often. You see I was in the midst of doing something I really love. I was speaking and doing what I call "Storypainting" (making large paintings very quickly and using them as the jumping off point for storytelling) at Haven Camp.

Haven Camp is a camp put on by Delta Lake Bible Conference in Rome, NY for adults with special needs. They do the camp about eight times a year and it is phenomenal. I've been their speaker four times in the last few years and I love it. The campers are always fun and endearing and I always have a great time working with them. They are some of the most open hearted people you will ever meet and I always come away from the experience on a joy filled, Spirit filled "high."

The idea for this book came from the camp director, Steve Clark. He had asked me to think about creating a piece of art for the next year's overall camp theme. This would be the theme not just for Haven, but for the multitude of other camps they do in the year. I, of course, jumped at the chance because I love this camp and what they do. The thing is, I was stuck. I thought the theme sounded good, but for some reason the ideas were slow in coming, and slow is me being charitable. I was at a loss–totally blank. I sat down with Steve and he said he was rethinking the idea. It was a one word theme and that word had become associated with a contro-versial event that was happening in the news. The controversy had nothing to do with the direction he wanted to take, but he thought it might prove to be a distraction, so he was working through a new idea. Another one word title...

"Enough."

Well this was different, where the first idea left me blocked, this one hit me with a virtual torrent of ideas. From the moment he said the word, the idea center of my brain (or more likely the Spirit of God in my heart) went onto overdrive. I was having idea after idea after idea. What does it mean to have enough? What does it mean to be enough? When have I done enough? When is it time to say "enough's enough?" and perhaps most importantly for the Christian, "Is Christ enough?" I soon knew this was going to be a lot more than a simple illustration or even a speaking series. This thing was fast becoming a book, and maybe more.

This topic was near and dear to my heart. Growing up, I always felt like I was never enough? As a result I found myself in a state of depression most of the time. As I went through life, I always felt like I didn't measure up. Added to this is the fact that many of my peers seemed bent on proving to me this was true. I was not enough and I was pretty sure I would never be enough. Yes, I was one of those human target kids. When I graduated from high school, I had a huge chip on my shoulder and I felt like I had to "show them all." I became an artist, and I jumped in with both feet. I worked full time in a variety of mostly graphic design jobs and took a plethora of other jobs and any freelance work I could get. I worked most of my waking hours. During this time, I met my wife, came to faith in Christ, married, had children and my quest to be enough was taking it's toll. I had landed a freelance job working for a licensee of the Teenage Mutant Ninja Turtles. I was convinced that this would be the thing to launch my career. When my wife confronted me about how much I was working, I told her one day soon I would "make it, and when I did, I would be able to give her everything she could ever want. The thing is those weren't her demands, they were mine. She just wanted a sane husband, I'm the only one who thought I wasn't enough, but when I "made" it, when I hit that level of success, then I would be enough. That's what I thought, but I was lying to myself.

The thing about "enough" is it changes, and it's slippery. About the time you think you've reached that magic status you call "enough," you'll see something just beyond the horizon and before you know it, "enough" has moved further down the line. I was on a hamster wheel and it was time to get off. I was close to destroying everything good in my life, when, I believe, God intervened. In His own way and in His own time, He showed me that, in Him, I was already enough, that I had enough, and most importantly that He is enough. I'd like to share what I've learned with you.

This book is for anyone who think's they're not enough, or thinks they don't have enough or maybe even wrestles with whether or not they will ever be enough. The answer is simple. In Christ, you are enough, because in anything you lack, He will be enough.

Introduction

I heard the story once of a very famous author. I won't give his name in case the story isn't true (the principle works regardless), but he's a name you would know. He was at a dinner party when a friend pointed out a very young, 25ish man. The friend said, "You see that guy over there? He'll make more money this year, than all your books together have ever made."

The author replied, "...but I have something he'll never have..."

"Enough."

It's true. For many of us, "enough" is an elusive thing. It's a sliding scale, a moving target, an unreachable goal, made unreachable by our own growing desires. Put simply, "enough is tough."

People often say that life is a journey, and it's true. In that journey we have times where the travel is smooth. Things go well and, as the song says, "the livin' is easy," but then there are those other times. There are times where we face obstacles that seem insurmountable. These obstacles seem like large mountains and the size of them make us feel small and in-significant, like we're nothing more than a little dot. It's more than resources—more than just money and possessions. It can manifest in virtually every aspect of life. In some ways, when taken to the lowest common denominator, it seems to come down to a question, "Am I enough?" Isn't that really what this quest for enough is all about? Do we have what it takes? Are we good enough? It's a question of value, and of questioning of our value. These questions can put us on the hamster wheel of self-fulfillment, running hard and getting nowhere fast. Maybe it's time to say, "Enough's enough!"

Add to this the element of Christian faith and we come to an even more profound question—one many of us would just as soon sweep under a rug. "Is Jesus enough?" Oh we sing songs that say "Your Grace is Enough" or "All of You is More Than Enough" but in the quiet moments is the All-Sufficient One really enough for you?

The good news is, whether you realize it or not, whether you accept it or not, He is enough. He is all you will ever really need and He has everything you will ever really need and it is in embracing His "enough-ness" (like that word? I just made it up!) that we find real life and real peace, not to mention purpose and value.

So step off the hamster wheel and join me as we explore what it means to be and to have enough in the One who is truly more than enough. After all you were made for more than the closed system of the hamster cage with tubes and diversions, but no real purpose. You were made for freedom and life, by the One who created freedom and life. In Him, you are enough.

1
What Is Enough?
Exploring Materialism

Let's start with stuff. One of the chief areas where people wrestle with enough is in the area of having enough. Enough money, enough material wealth, enough of the status that seems to come with the stuff. As I'm sure you probably already have figured out, the mater of "enough" is a sliding scale. Every time you think you have enough, someone comes out with something newer or better and as a result, contentment is elusive. Consider your cell phone...

Up until I was at the end of my junior year in high school I had only one plan (at least one I stuck to). I wanted to be an artist. Now when you're a six year old and you tell your parents you want to be an artist, they pat you on the head and say, "That's nice Davy, now go play with your crayons." When you're heading into your senior year of high school and you're still saying you want to be an artist, they start to panic, or at least my folks did. "You know most artists never make a living at it." they would say and I would say, "Yes, but I still want to do it." "But what if you don't succeed?" "I will," I replied. Their final shot across the bow was "No son of ours is going to starve in an attic! Pick something else." Well by now, I was starting to panic. What if they were right? (They weren't. My near constant struggle with weight shows that, at the very least, they were wrong on the "starving" front.) Regardless, I gave in, and with one year left in high school I started to seek out the new plan.

Engineer Without Aptitude

One day in my senior year, a sales rep from a tech school came into our class. He told us of their three year degree program and the high pays that some of their graduates were receiving and I was hooked. Remember, I wanted to show

15

them all. If I went to this school, I would be making a great living while my oppressors were still flipping burgers and trying to finish college. "Yessiree, I'm going to become an electronics engineer. That'll show them." Forget the fact that I had no experience or aptitude for the subject matter, and no real knowledge of what an electronics engineer does. When I became one, I would be enough. Well needless to say that whole thing fell apart pretty quickly, but back to phones.

The computer in the school I went to, yes there was one and only one, (it was the early eighties after all). It was a huge mainframe, it filled an entire large room and fed terminals all over the building. I mention that because of this. The iPhone 7 I carry in my pocket right at this moment, has more computing power than that giant mainframe did when I was in school. It's an amazing device that can connect me with the world in amazing ways, but guess what. They just came out with the iPhone 10 and the seven is, for many people, no longer enough. Enough changes rapidly. Get caught up in the "enoughness" of materialism and you will be trapped.

Jesus and Bigger Barns
Jesus often taught in stories called parables and we will look at several of them in this volume. The parables held a two-fold purpose. The secondary purpose would take a lot of time to discuss and dealt with people who were hard-hearted and didn't want to receive God's truth. I'm going to make the assumption that you would not be reading this book if you were one of them and so we will deal with the primary purpose. Jesus' primary reason for teaching in parables was to help open-hearted believers to understand truth. They were simple stories, and most people believe that, rather than being true stories, they were illustrations, similar to your pastor's sermon illustrations, designed to help those seeking truth to understand.

In this particular story, found in Luke 12:16-21, Jesus speaks of a rich man who was blessed beyond measure. He was a farmer, though one could probably imagine he is not merely a subsistence farmer, growing what he needs to live. Rather, this is a "land baron" type, with many, many acres and a large operation. I say this, at least in part, because most translations of the Bible title this story something to the effect of, *The Parable of the Rich Fool.* We'll call him MacDonald, for obvious reasons.

MacDonald's farm has been quite productive this year. He planted well, at just the right time. Well most likely his servants and hired men planted, but you get the point. Now, as you are probably aware, farming can be a fairly fickle enterprise. A whole lot of factors have to come together to make a good crop, and doing everything right is no guarantee of success. A whole lot of things can go wrong in farming. It's not surprising that many farmers are people of faith, because they realize how much of their livelihood depends on the Lord's provision, even in the midst of all their hard work.

Well for MacDonald, everything lined up, the Lord provided, and the crop was amazing, generating much more than MacDonald had ever had before. In farming, this is what they call a good problem. He has more blessings than he can handle, and more than he can use. What will he do? He's got a lot of food and nowhere to go with it. Then MacDonald gets a brainstorm. "I know what I'll do. I'll tear down my perfectly good barns and build bigger ones. Then I'll have plenty of room to store up everything I've been given and I'll be able to live off of it for years. No more work," he thought. "From this point on, I can eat, drink, and be merry."

Now please remember this is a parable, an illustration, and I don't want to take it too far, but think about this for a moment. There is considerable folly in what he is doing here. Yes, he can store the crops and bigger barns will be helpful to that end, but the thing about agricultural products is they have a shelf life. He can store them for a while, but not for the many years he speaks of. Sooner or later, especially in the pre-preservative days when Jesus walked the earth, the stuff is going to start to rot. It's not going to last forever and this is at least part of Jesus' point.

About the time, that MacDonald had his thought, he heard from God. God said basically, "You fool, you're going to die tonight. Then who will get what you have saved for yourself?" This is the danger of trusting in stuff. Life is simply not predictable and if we place our trust in our stuff, we need to know it will never be enough.

Checking the Context

When looking at a parable, because it is an illustration, it's often helpful to look at the context (If context is provided) to see to whom Jesus is talking. In this way, we can at least begin to discern why Jesus told the story. In this particular case, Luke gives us the background in verses 13-15. Jesus was teaching when a man in the crowd came up to Him and asked Him, actually more like ordered Him, to tell the man's brother to divide their inheritance between them. This was hardly what Jesus was there for. The man was probably hoping that Jesus would use the considerable authority Rabbi's had, to push the man's brother to do the right thing, at least from the man's perspective. Jesus' mission was so much bigger than material things. It still is.

Jesus took the man to task, basically saying, "Who made me the judge? Be on your guard against greed, your life is more than what you have." This was the background for the parable. The man was obviously more concerned with his inheritance than he was with his relationship with his own brother. Material things were causing problems in their relationship and this parable is designed as a warning. How many times have we seen families divided over money and things? How many time have we seen communities and even churches divided over money and resources? This should never be. God's material blessings are important, but people are more important. We weren't created for things, we were created for relationships.

A Blessing Becomes a Curse

I once heard the story of a church that received an end-of-life donation of 500.000 dollars. I was a new pastor when I heard the story and I assumed the story would end happily. Surely those kinds of resources allowed the church to do some incredible things, and I'll confess my mind started to wander into all the wonderful, Kingdom building things my fledgling church could do with 500,000 dollars. I was shocked back to reality by the rest of the story. You see the church split and nearly died because of the gift. Rather than seeing it as a blessing, the congregation began to divide over how to best use their windfall. I'm sure the person who left them the money was rolling in their grave (if that's a thing and it isn't) over that one. What was intended to be a blessing, ended up being a curse.

Bumper Crops of Blessings

That word "blessing" is the key. Every good thing we have is a blessing from God, not unlike MacDonald's bumper crop. The bequest to the church was also a blessing from God. Both things were given for the good of the people who would receive the blessing. That's why it's called a "blessing." I know some might be tempted to throw out that mistranslated verse, "Money is the root of all evil," and both the parable and the true church story seem to bear it out, except that's not what the Bible says. The Bible says "the love of money is the root of all evil." (1 Timothy 6:10 NIV) You see the problem is not in the gift, the gift is good and it comes from a good God, No the problem is in the heart of the receiver.

19

Hoarding Isn't Stewardship

When God blesses us, He primarily blesses us so that we have the resources to be a blessing. MacDonald's bumper crop would have rotted in the barn long before he could have used it all. Note that Jesus does not condemn MacDonald for storing some of the grain in his existing barns, and saving is good stewardship. The problem wasn't saving, it was hoarding and a lack of faith. It was as if MacDonald was saying, "God had provided this time, but what if He doesn't provide again? I better keep it all." Is this how you treat God's blessing? MacDonald wasn't given a bumper crop for it to be hoarded, and it surely wasn't given so he would wastefully destroy perfectly good barns. It wasn't given so the crop would sit in a barn and rot. No, the idea was fill your barn and be a blessing with what's left. Help the poor and the needy. Love your neighbor by feeding your neighbor.

What If?

MacDonald's scarcity mentality made him greedy and I believe that same mentality is always near to our hearts. We're not sure God will continue to be good and so we better make sure we keep all that we've been given. We may not say that in so many words, but that's what a scarcity mindset reveals What we need to understand is the data behind that mindset is flawed. God is persistently good and He always provides. When we trust God to be good, we can be generous. If we decide to place our trust in our possessions, we will never have enough. "What if?" scenarios will keep us on a quest for more and more "material security." Don't buy into that. Our trust is in Christ alone.

Possessions are lifeless and cannot be trusted. Further, remember, Jesus is telling this story as a way of showing two brothers that their priorities are in the wrong place. Money and possessions are nowhere near as important as the relationships we have with the people we love. People must always come before possessions. Trusting in God will show us, we have more than enough and when we know we have more than enough, and that our source is trustworthy, we will become generous. When we become generous, our possessions begin to occupy the proper place in our lives. We are blessed to be a blessing and when we fall into that mindset, more blessings equal greater opportunities to bless. I believe this is the heart of God for our possessions.

The church from our story would have been far better off giving all the money away. To divide a church over what is ostensibly a blessing from God, shows major problems in the hearts of the people. What good could have been done if they had come together in prayer, offered their blessing back to the Lord and submitted to His plan for blessing those around them? Instead we have the tragic story of a fractured church and a misused blessing.

How is your relationship with possessions? Do you live in a scarcity mentality or do you trust in God to provide? A lot of that can be told by your answer to a question. "Do you have enough?" Now to be sure, I don't know your circumstances. Perhaps you are in a place of genuine need. None of this is meant to be a put down of you or your circumstances. It is simply a discussion of priority and my prayer for you is two-fold. First, that God would bless you, perhaps through someone else who has been blessed to be a blessing, and secondly that when you receive that blessing, you too will be a blessing. When it comes to material possessions, enough is found in holding on tightly to God and loosely to your possessions.

The Secret to Contentment
The apostle Paul seemed to have this all pretty well figured out. In writing to the church he founded in Philippi, Paul wrote:

"I am not saying this because I am in need, for I have learned to be content whatever the circumstances."

Now there is something we could all use, right? Paul was content in all circumstances, literally. He continues:

"I know what it is to be in need, and I know what it is to have plenty. I have learned the secret of being content in any and every situation, whether well fed or hungry, whether living in plenty or in want."

Please note, Paul is not content because things are always good. Sometimes there are bumper crops, other times it's "slim pickin's" but Paul has learned the secret to being content no matter what? How could he have all this contentment? He knew what we need to know:

"I can do all this through him who gives me strength." (Philippians 4:11-13 NIV)

There it is. The secret to contentment, the secret to "enough" in the material world and beyond—Whether well fed or hungry, rich, poor, in need or in want, or whatever, we need an abiding trust in the One through whom we can do all things. As long as God is with him, Paul has everything he needs to do whatever he needs to do, and to get his needs met. He trusts God to provide and because of that, he has enough.

Maybe this is why Jesus reminded us "Do not store up for yourselves treasures on earth, where moths and vermin destroy, and where thieves break in and steal. But store up for yourselves treasures in heaven, where moths and vermin do not destroy, and where thieves do not break in and steal. For where your treasure is, there your heart will be also."(Matthew 6:19-21 NIV)

There is a place where the treasures of our generosity acrue a kind of eternal inheritance. That place is heaven, and we're not there yet. Here on earth, we are blessed to be a blessing.

No need to build bigger barns, because we can't take it with us. You'll never see a hearse pulling a U-Haul trailer. It is far better to use God's blessings for what we need and be a blessing with the rest. Because of the finished work of Jesus on the cross, where we believers are headed, we won't need our earthly stuff, so it's better to share what we have here. Maybe if we do, some will see a little of God's goodness in our lives and want to know Jesus, so they can join us there.

The key to contentment with what we have, is to trust it all to the One who will always be enough.

2
Am I Enough?
Exploring Self-worth

This whole quest begins with a question: "Am I enough?" This is at the core of the quest of every person seeking to be enough, however that manifests in life. For some it's the quest for stuff and status, for others power and privilege, and for some it manifests in truly ugly ways—the quest to dominate, overpower and do harm. It will cause people to pad their resume's, lie, cheat and steal. It will cause some people to reach for the stars and other people to race to the bottom.

The One Who Dies With the Most Toys...

When I was a kid, I used to wear a button that said "The one who dies with the most toys wins." It was both amusing and tragic. Was that really where I found my value? Was that what it would take for me to be enough? Sadly for a long time it was. The most miserable day of my life to that point, was the day I turned thirty. I should have been happy. I had a great wife, a wonderful son and it was mere days until another son would be born. I had a new home and much to be grateful for, Instead I was miserable. "Why?" you might ask. I wasn't a millionaire and I had sworn to myself that I would be. I was the guy who had something to prove and I wanted to show them all. As I look back, I have to ask two questions? "Show who all?" and "Show them what?"

The who was easy. This mythical group of people that had said, either by their words or by their actions, that I would never be anything, but the what was harder. I now know the truth. What I wanted to show "them" was that I was enough. That I had value, that I was important, that my life mattered. The thing is their lives had moved on, and they weren't thinking of me at all. No the person I was really trying to show was me. I didn't think I measured up. I didn't think I mattered. The evidence this was false was all around me, but I felt like I needed something more.

Maybe you need to know this too. The people you think you need to show, have most likely moved on and it's not likely they think about you at all anymore. That might be hard to hear, but it's likely the truth. They don't care about you. If they did they wouldn't have treated you that way in the first place. Since this is likely the case, can I give you a bit of incredibly good news? You're free. You can move on. You can be the best you you can be. On the slim chance that they're still in your life, can I ask you a question? Why do you care? Think about what you're doing. You're giving them power over your life. Power they've already proven they don't deserve. Not only that, but you're doing it at the expense of the people who love and care about you. You're actually depriving the people you love of your time, while you're trying to prove something to people who wouldn't cross the street for you. It makes no sense.

There's a Better Way

I know this to be true. While I thought I was trying to prove something to people who long ago gave up any interest in me at all, my loving family was missing me. Oh I thought I was doing all this for them. While I was chasing the impossible dream, I would have said that I was doing it so that I could give them everything they ever wanted, but what they really wanted were things that I already had the capacity to give them. They wanted a husband and father in a stable home. If any of this is ringing true with you, you need to know there is a better way.

So let's go back to the original question, "Are you enough?" The answer is yes and the answer is no, and both of those are very good news. Let's start with the yes. As a man of faith, I have come to believe that God has provided us with everything we need to accomplish the plans and purposes He has for our lives. Now please note the word "need." I wanted a million dollars and here we are decades later and I am still nowhere close. I wanted it, but I didn't need it and when I gave up pursuing what I wanted, I found I already had what I needed. I had work and a home and a family who loved me. I didn't need "more. I needed to learn to appreciate what God had already given and I had to learn how to be faithful with it. I had to learn I had enough and I was enough. I read a saying on a church sign once that said, "Do what you can, with what you have, where you are." Okay it was my church sign, but I didn't put it there, My friend Lucy, who does our sign put it there. As I crested the hill to go to my office on a Wednesday morning, there it was and as I read it, I realized that's the key to contentment and having and being enough.

The quest for enough was brutal on my life. It's part of the reason I'm sitting in a Sheetz convenience store banging away on my iMac right now. I want every person to read these stories and take a different path. I want you, dear reader, to be encouraged. I want you to realize that you are in many ways enough, right where you are, right now, today. I want you to know that you are loved by God and you can be everything that God has created you to be, no exceptions.

Where You're Not Enough
Now, if you were paying attention above, my answer to the question "Am I enough?" was both "yes" and "no." Where does the "no" come from? Well there are areas of life where you are not enough, and this too is by design. You see, I believe with all my heart that we are created by God on purpose for a purpose, and yes, with no apologies, you will read that several more times in this book. You will also read in this book, that part of God's design in our creation, perhaps the greatest part, is that you were created for relationship. First of all you were created to be in relationship with Him. God made you for the purpose of loving you and conversely for you to love Him. This is huge and we will explore it in

greater detail in later chapters, but we were also created to be in relationship with other human beings.

We're a Body

In 1 Corinthians 12, the Apostle Paul speaks of the church being the body of Christ and in the process he touches on my primary point here. This is one of the two reasons we should all be grateful that we are not enough. You see Paul relates the church to a literal body and in that body, each part has a special, by design, function. He speaks of eyes that want to be ears and hands that want to be feet, and asks where the head would be without the feet, which gives me this humorous image of a whole bunch of sentient, disembodied heads rolling around aimlessly wishing for a pair of feet to get them where they know they need to be. It's humorous, but it's precisely the point. The head might do all the thinking, but the head needs the feet, and the arms and the legs and without them, his life is more difficult.

You see here in the 21st century, at least in the west, we are taught from an extremely early age to value independence, and value it highly. We salute things like rugged individualism and admire "self-made" people greatly. In some ways that is a great thing, but it's not God's ultimate design. First of all there is no such thing as a "self-made" person. You're made by God, period and rugged individuals are setting themselves up for failure. No one can do it all. No, God's ultimate design for us is not independence, it's interdependence. He designed us with strengths and weaknesses precisely for this reason. No man, over woman, is an island and this too is by design. We were created to depend on each other and in this sense we are not enough on our own.

My Better Half

I have a great example of this in my wife Dawn. I'm a natural born artist/creative. This means my imagination is usually fully engaged. I am right brained to the extreme and my brain seems to malfunction around things like numbers and money. So you know what God did for me? He gave me a wife who is great a crunching numbers and He gave me the wisdom to let her handle the finances. As a result we have stupid things like the aforementioned roof over our heads. I am not a starving artist because of the goodness of my God and the wisdom of my wife. She helps to ground me a bit and I help her to free up her inborn creativity. It's a win-win situation. She is strong where I am weak and I am strong in her areas of weakness and together it works. I get a little nauseous when I hear someone in one of those chick flicks look someone in the eye and say "You complete me!" but to some degree it's true, and it is God's design.

And by the way, it's not just in marriages. The same principle works in families and companies and churches and communities and even nations. If we were all to accept the idea that we are not in and of ourselves "enough" and learn to bring our best to the table in our areas of strength, in cooperation with those who are strong in our weaknesses, the world would be a much better, more efficient, place. We need to love others, work in our strengths and cooperate with others, until we are all, together, enough.

Total Dependence
Of course there is an area where independence will not work and where even interdependence falls short and that is in our relationship with God. You see, He wants us to be totally dependent on Him and we are. I had an awakening on this one day. I had written a message where I said "God takes care of us in everything from the air we breathe on up." But then I really thought about it, "Without air, where are we?" Air isn't just a need, it's our primary need and God provides it, and everything else, in abundance. There is nothing in our world that, when brought down to it's lowest common denominator, is not totally and completely dependent on God. If this is the case, and it is, then when it comes to God, none

of us is enough. We are totally and completely dependent on Him and that is incredibly good news, because He is forever unchanging and totally dependable to us. He is totally and completely enough and He is all we will ever really need.

It gets even better. While we are totally dependent on God, we are also immensely valuable to Him. It's not that He needs us, It's that He desires us. He wants to be in relationship with us. The question of "Am I enough?" is ultimately a question of value. God answers the question in Romans 5:8 (NIV) where He, through the Apostle Paul, says, "But God demonstrates his own love for us in this: While we were still sinners, Christ died for us."

Do you catch the meaning in that? God so completely loves you, that He gave His only Son to die in your place, so that your relationship with Him would be eternal. We'll discuss this more in the coming chapters but for now suffice it to say, if "Am I enough?" is a question of value, this verse, and most of the teachings of Scripture, shows that your value to the One who matters most is extremely high. So I would say that God would answer the question of your enough-ness with a qualified yes. I believe He would say, "You are enough for what I have created you to be and do. In any areas where you are not enough, I have placed people in your life so that you can be enough together and finally you are totally dependent on me, so in all things, trust me to be enough."

Trust Him to be enough and be enough in Him!

3
Am I Important Enough?
Do I Matter?

Hopefully as you read this book you will become increasingly aware that I am not a person under any illusions that I have it all together. I don't. If you want a book written by someone perfect, read the Bible. You should be reading that anyway! That being said, this is one of the areas where I have always struggled most and my guess is, I'm not the only one. This pursuit was especially bad back in the proving myself days, but the srtruggle can still manifest even in this fairly contented phase of life. I can still find myself asking questions of significance. Does what I'm doing really matter? Could I be doing more or gaining more or even having more of a Kingdom impact? Am I important? Does any of this even matter? Can I tell you those are the wrong questions? I would like to illustrate this by telling you a story.

Do Not Despise Small Beginnings

I was heading to a Promise Keepers event in Philadelphia and I was exhausted. Driving down the Schuylkill Expressway (locals call it the "Sure kill" because it just might be the worst road in the U.S.) and I was fading fast. I still had a two to three hour event ahead of me, and then what could be another two to three hour drive at the end, depending on how bad the traffic was on the aforementioned "Sure kill." A thought was running through my mind as I hoped the caffeine from my Mountain Dew would kick in. "The first speaker better 'bring it' or I am going to fall asleep." Well the first speaker that night was a man named E.V. Hill. He stepped up to the microphone and began to speak. He started off speaking very slowly and deliberately and I was beginning to think, "Oh no, I am in trouble." Well I should have known better, because he kept building intensity and volume, until by the end, he was all but screaming and I was on the edge of my seat. I didn't want it to end. He was probably among the best preachers I have ever heard. I was excited—so excited, that I told everyone I could, that they had to hear this amazing preacher.

Well the next year, Promise Keepers came to town again and when they came, they brought E.V. Hill with them. I had a car load of friends going with me and I could not wait for them to hear Reverend Hill bring God's Word. I couldn't believe what happened next. He started boasting. Boasting about this accomplishment and that accomplishment and this great thing he did, and that great place he went, and the literal millions of people he had spoken to, and the more he boasted, the more I sunk down in my chair. I could almost feel my friends staring me down and thinking "What's so great about this guy?" Again, I should have known better.

You see round about the middle of the message, Reverend Hill began to speak about the pastor at his first church—the first church he attended—the one where he met the Lord. He told us, that pastor had never preached to more than 70 people in his life, but if he had not been faithful to his call, all the great things God used E.V. Hill to do, might never have happened. The point is simple. "Big enough" and it's sister "important enough" aren't up to us, faithfulness is. The question is not the importance of our actions the question is how faithful will we be with the opportunities God gives us?

Faithfulness Flourishes

Another example. Have you ever heard of Mordecai Hamm? I'm guessing most of my readers would say "no," so let me ask you another question. Have you ever heard of Billy Graham (I'm writing this on his 99th birthday)? Of course you probably have. He may have been the greatest evangelist of the 20th century. Millions of people came to a saving knowledge of Jesus Christ under his ministry. Well if you've heard of Billy Graham, or if you believe in the impact that

God had through him, you might want to say a little prayer thanking God for Mordecai Hamm. The reason is simple, Mordecai Hamm was the evangelist preaching the night Billy Graham came to Christ. No Mordecai Hamm and (maybe) no Billy Graham. Hamm's ministry was not world famous like his successor's was, but because he served in faithfulness, Millions were reached through a man Hamm was used to reach.

Our importance is not measured by the "bigness" of what we do. It's measured by the faithfulness by which we do what God puts before us. The question is not "Are you important enough?" or "Are you big enough?" The question is "Are you faithful enough?"

Learning The Hard Way

I saw this happen in my own life. I got the call to ministry when I was the 35 years old. My first ministry was as the youth leader in a small church here in Pennsylvania. It was small but I was learning, and it was growing, and I loved it. Around five years into that I began to really feel the call to plant a church. We started with eight people. We did almost everything the experts say not to do, and made almost every mistake in the book and still we grew but only to about 30 people. It was a good time and a hard time, but for ow I want to focus on the hardest part. The end part.

We labored there for ten years. Toward the end, the church started to fade, and eventually the church closed. So much for my first pastorate, and of course the enemy of my soul was right there, saying things like, "You call your self a pastor? You're a failure and a loser and a whole bunch of other things." For the record, I was really tempted to go along with it. I was down and out and feeling terrible. I had failed… or had I? One day the Lord reminded me about three people who dedicated their lives to Christ as Lord and Savior during that time and there was a new question to be asked. "Were those three people (and there may have been more) spending life in paradise for eternity, worth ten years of my life?" The answer was "Yes!"

When it comes to the Kingdom of God, I don't think we human beings can understand success and failure or big and small or the real impact of our actions. Maybe that's why Zechariah 4:10 (NIV) says, "Do not despise these small beginnings, for the Lord rejoices to see the work begin…" Don't sweat the small stuff, but don't be afraid to do the small stuff. The size of our results is really beyond our control anyway. What we are responsible for is our own faithfulness. So if you're wondering if you're big enough or important enough, all I can say is if you're being faithful, that's enough.

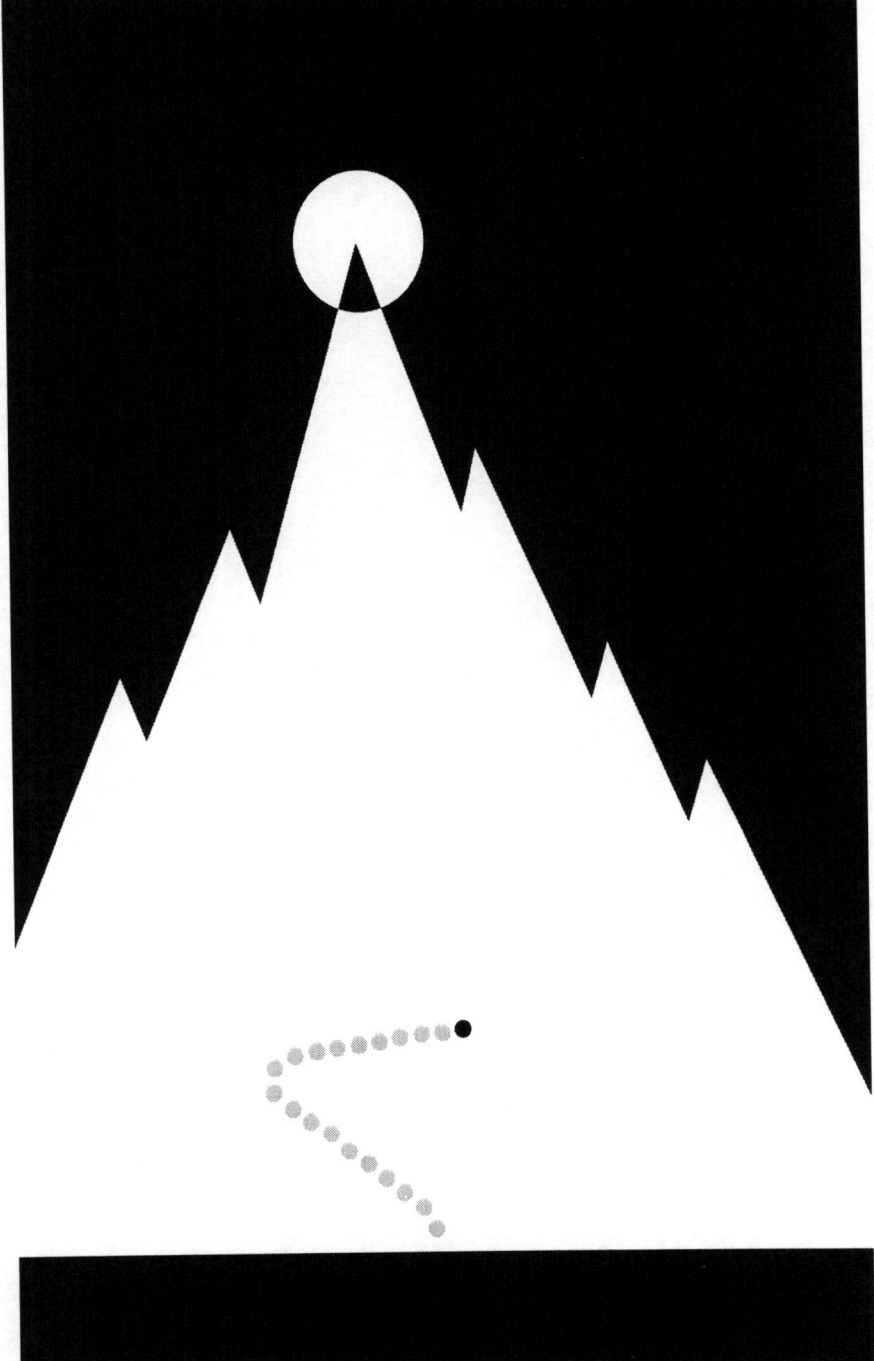

4
Am I Good Enough?
Exploring Righteousness and Salvation

Generally there are two ways people struggle with righteousness. They either overestimate or they underestimate their own righteousness. Let me set the record straight. If you wonder if you're good enough to be saved, I can tell you. You're not. That's the bad news, the slightly better news is you're not alone. You see, neither is anyone else. In Romans 3:10-12, Paul reminds us, "None is righteous, no, not one; no one understands; no one seeks for God. All have turned aside; together they have become worthless; no one does good, not even one." (NIV) Later in the same chapter, Paul takes this thought to its logical conclusion. "All have sinned and fall short of the glory of God." (Romans 3:23 NIV)

People who wish to overestimate their own righteousness have a habit of getting this really wrong and it's really easy to do. They just start to look for someone who is doing worse than they are, or committing different sins than they are, because human nature always seems to say, "The worst sins are the ones I am not committing." No for all intents and purposes, sin is sin. All sins are wrong and all of them separate us from a perfect God. Let's face it, everyone on earth can find someone who is worse than they are, if they look hard enough. Well okay, there's that one guy who is the absolute worse, but the rest of the seven billion are somewhere in the middle. Find that one person and you start to feel better about yourself. "I'm not perfect, but I'm better than so and so." That may be, but so and so is not the standard. God is and Jesus is, and the standard is perfection.

Peter reminds us of Leviticus 11:44, which commands us to be holy as God is holy. Jesus, in the sermon on the mount, told us to be perfect as our heavenly Father is perfect. God is the standard and no one else. Unless you're perfect, and no one but Jesus is, you're not good enough, at least not for heaven, at least not on your own. If you're a person who overestimates your own righteousness, I have bad news, you're not good enough. Stick with me, though, I'll have some good news.

But first I need to talk to the rest of you. The ones who underestimate yourself and think you'll never be good enough. You see everyone as better than you, and you look at your chances as pretty hopelessly. First off, you need to read the previous chapter, but stay here for now. You see, you already have something going for you that the previously mentioned people can't seem to find. It's called humility. You see a command to be holy like God, and you know in your heart, you can't. You see Jesus calling you to be perfect like God, and you might even want to, but you know you fall short. Believe it or not, you're already halfway to where you need to be. Where the proud person wants to self justify by comparing himself to someone who might be sinning more than they are, you see your imperfection and know self justification is impossible for you. You stick with me too, because I have great news for you.

The Tax Collector and the Pharisee
Jesus told a story in Luke 18 about two men at the temple. Both came to pray, and again this is a parable, an illustration and not a true story, but a story told to prove a point. Remember too, that to really understand a parable, you should look to see who Jesus is teaching. In this case, it is pretty simple. In the first verse of the story, Luke tells us Jesus is speaking to the people who are convinced that they are good and righteous—people with their noses permanently in the air, looking down on everyone else. This may very well be a group of Pharisees since they were experts in the law and convinced they were better at keeping the law than anyone else. They also persistently opposed Jesus. The other reason I am pretty

sure Jesus is talking to Pharisees is because He flat out says the first character in His story is a Pharisee. The Pharisee takes center stage. He stands for the world to see and thanks God that he is not a sinner like the people around him. And then he lays out his list—the list of people he is better than: Thieves, evildoers and adulterers. Now before we go on, is this really even a prayer? It seems to me it's not. It's a performance for the people around him. He's standing there before men and saying essentially, "Hey look at me. Here's a list of the people I'm better than," and the implication is "and I'm better than you too!" Make no mistake about it, this kind of prayer is not pleasing to God.

In Matthew 6, Jesus said, "Be careful not to perform your righteous acts before men to be seen by them. If you do, you will have no reward from your Father in heaven. So when you give to the needy, do not sound a trumpet before you, as the hypocrites do in the synagogues and on the streets, to be praised by men. Truly I tell you, they already have their reward." (NIV) The point is simple. If you do your Spiritual things so that people will see them and think more highly of you, enjoy the accolades, because that is all you will ever get out of it, and you will certainly not receive the reward God has for you.

The Pharisee's prayer is not a prayer, it's a farce, but he's not done. Next he starts to talk about his giving, (Remember what Jesus said above?) and about his fasting, which we're also supposed to do without a lot of fanfare. The reason we're not supposed to boast about ourselves, or our prayer or any other Spiritual disciplines is very simple. What we do for God is supposed to be between us and God, not to shore up the opinions of men. Is this Pharisee trying to show the world that he is enough? It sure feels like he is, because it seems like he has something to prove. It's not enough for him to strive for righteousness, which we should do, or even to think he is righteous, no, he wants to show everyone that he is righteous. I get the idea from the tone of the parable that no one is fooled, least of all Jesus.

I deliberately left one person from the list of people the Pharisee felt himself to be better than, and that is the man standing next to him, the other character in Jesus' story, the tax collector. This proud Pharisee actually stands next to another human being and says in effect, "Thank you God that I'm not a sinner like him." Now the other man was a tax collector and the tax collectors were almost universally hated in Jesus' day. They were seen as turncoats against their own people and stooges of the Roman government, the hated oppressors of the people, well at least the common people. You got to be a tax collector by bidding for the job, and, as it still is today with many government contracts, the job usually goes to the lowest bidder. The thing is they could afford to bid fairly low, because many tax collectors would make up any losses by ripping off the taxpayers. Again remember this Pharisee is a made-up character in an illustration story told by Jesus, but consider how Jesus sets up the story. The first main character was a Pharisee, a man who would have been held in high regard by the people, largely because a the Pharisees had almost everyone convinced they were righteous. By comparison the second main character, the tax collector, was someone the people in Jesus' audience would have found reprehensible and irredeemable.

What happens next is a masterful study in contrasts. While the Pharisee prays at center stage, the tax collector stands at a distance. While the Pharisee stands for all to see, the tax collector can't even bring himself to look up toward heaven. While the Pharisee boasts of his piety, the tax collector beat his breast. While the Pharisee thanks God for his own goodness, the tax collector confesses and asks for mercy. "God, have mercy on me, a sinner." (Luke 18:13 NIV)

By now Jesus' original audience was probably not happy. The proud Pharisees would have seen this parable was not going their way, but if that didn't upset them, what Jesus said next definitely would have. "I tell you that this man, rather than the other, went home justified before God. For all those who exalt themselves will be humbled, and those who humble themselves will be exalted." (Luke 18:14 NIV) The message is simple. None of us are good enough. None of us can self-justify, try though we sometimes do. Our imperfections keep it from happening. On our own we are not good enough.

Now if you're prideful, you might not be too happy with me right now, and if you're stuck in shame, I haven't made you feel any better. Hold tight, we're almost there. None of us is righteous. None of us is perfect and if we start to think we are, Isaiah reminds us that our righteousness is about as good as a filthy rag. We're simply not good enough... on our own... but in Christ, we're not on our own. No, we're not good enough, we're not righteous, but in Christ we are made righteous. In Christ, as we are reminded in Romans 8, we are "more than conquerors." Then look what it says. 'If God is for us, who can be against us? He who did not spare his own Son, but gave him up for us all—how will he not also, along with him, graciously give us all things? Who will bring any charge against those whom God has chosen? It is God who justifies. Who then is the one who condemns? Christ Jesus who died—more than that, who was raised to life—is at the right hand of God and is also interceding for us." (Romans 8:31-34 NIV)

What this means is simple. You might not be righteous on your own, but you are loved by God and if He is for you, no one can stand against you. He loves you so much He gave His only Son for you and in Him you are made righteous. Who can bring a charge against you if God has chosen you? No one. Oh, there is One who could. The only One who is truly righteous, Jesus Christ. His righteousness could condemn your unrighteousness, but He is not condemning you because He is too busy praying for you and interceding for you. That is why the Scripture says "There is now no condemnation for those who are in Christ Jesus." (Romans 8:1 NIV) You might not have righteousness of your own, but if you are in Christ, if you belong to Jesus, you can wear His righteousness and be saved.

The Choice: Pride of Humility?

This leaves us with a choice, humility or pride? The choice should be easy, since we know God opposes the proud but gives grace to the humble. Opposing God is ultimately a fools errand and living in opposition to God is the surest way I can think of to ensure great loss and great failure. This brings us to something I would be remiss if I didn't share. Some might think that I am dismissing the importance of holiness and righteousness. Nothing could be further from the truth. So let me say it clearly, holiness and righteousness are of urgent importance in the life of every believer. After all, Jesus gave His life to pay the price for our sins. Surely we should not take that lightly. Further, how can God be glorified in our lives, if we claim the name of Christ and sin with abandon. To do such a thing should unthinkable in the life of a believer. So, are these thoughts contradictory? Which is it ? Do we try to be good enough or not? Well actually, it's kind of both.

Jesus said in Matthew 5:6 (NIV), "Blessed are those who hunger and thirst for righteousness, for they shall be filled." It sounds to me like Jesus is intent on the idea that we should be in a constant pursuit of righteousness and, in fact, this should be our pursuit. If we have died to our sins, we cannot continue to live in them, but again these statements are not contradictory. Rather we're dealing with a context issue and it all comes down to what we mean by "good enough." We could pursue righteousness from now until the day we leave this world and still not be good enough to receive, salvation.

Remember, salvation is a free gift from God. Our righteousness is not a matter of earning, because we are told very clearly that we are saved by grace and not by works. Nothing we do can earn salvation, so God gives it freely. We don't have to earn it, we're saved by grace through faith. Believe in Jesus and you're saved. Period. You're washed clean, you're made good enough in Jesus, not by your own efforts, but because He paid your price on the cross. The pursuit of righteousness is not about earning, it's about appreciation. Jesus gave His life for me. He laid down His life so that I can be free of my sin and spend eternity with Him in heaven. In effect, I'm not good enough and I never can be. I deserve nothing, but through Christ, I receive everything. There is only one logical response to "so great a salvation," and that is living a life of gratitude. Living to please the One who gave me so much.

Instant Billionaire

Suppose I gave you a billion dollars. For the record, I don't have a billion dollars, but imagine I do and I give it to you, unconditionally. It was mine and now it's yours, free and clear. It would radically change your life, right? (If a billion dollars would not radically change your life, please contact me, I have some really worthy projects I would love for you to support.) But seriously, if I benefitted you to that degree, and then one day you heard I wanted you to do something, I'm guessing you would do what I asked, right? I mean as long as that thing was moral, ethical and good, there should be very few things you wouldn't do for the one who so radically changed your life. Well everything Jesus has asked of us is good and ethical and moral, and He has given us something worth so much more than a billion dollars. He has given every believer a billion years and beyond in a perfect place of no more sickness and no more pain and no more disease, and no more death, and no Satan and no evil, just perfect joy and happiness forever. What He asks in return is that we live these few measly decades that we get on this planet in a way that brings Him honor and glory, so that others might seeh His gift in us and want it for themselves. If they receive Him, they receive eternity. That's what our attempts at lives of holiness and righteousness are really all about. Jesus came to rescue us and when He did, He assigned us to the rescue mission. We don't try to be good enough to earn something, we live to please Him so that others might receive Him and be saved.

So are you good enough? On your own, No! but in Him you are. From there we live in appreciation to the One who makes us good enough by putting His goodness on us. The choice is yours. Live to please the One in whom you are made good enough.

Enough

5
Am I Smart Enough?
Intelligence Versus Wisdom

I was extremely insecure. I had been for years. You see I never finished my degree. When college fell through, I started hustling to be an artist. I worked nearly constantly. I was a husband and father and in that phase of life, I really only had time for family and work. I gave up on getting a degree and it took a toll. When I entered my chosen field, I had been passed over many times, even a few times when I was probably better qualified, through experience, than my less experienced, but degreed competitors. When I got my call to ministry, I went into a denominational training program for second career ministers. It was great and I learned a lot, but it offered only a certificate and ordination, still no degree. Even though it was the denomination's program, the denominational pay scale made it clear, my education was second class. I didn't mind in a way, I was still ordained and NO ONE does ministry for the money, but when it came time to pastor a church, I was still a little intimidated by the more educated, occasionally with near disastrous results. I wondered, "Am I really smart enough to do this?"

Before I go any further, I want to make something really clear. I am not at all anti-education or anti-intellectual. I have since gotten one degree and am working on another. I think those of us entrusted with bringing people the Word of God should be constantly increasing our knowledge of the Word. I do however believe that we have to realize that the primary source of wisdom is the Word of God and if education, even theological education, contradicts the teachings of the Word of God, and much education does, that education is counterproductive. Intelligence is extremely important but wisdom is even more so.

The Smartest Man In the World?

I'm reminded of wise King Solomon. Here was a guy who had a great start. He was the king to follow the man who might have been the greatest king in the history of the world, King David. Solomon, as his heir, was faced with a massive challenge, to carry on the work of the "man after God's own heart." Knowing he was young and inexperienced, he was faced with a choice from God. God gave him something of a blank check. God said, "Ask for whatever you want me to give you." Solomon could have asked for anything in the world, but what He asked for was something that pleased God. He asked God for wisdom. God was so pleased with Solomon's request that He not only made Solomon incredibly wise, but He also gave him basically everything else he could have asked for, but didn't. Solomon became amazingly wealthy and his wisdom was sought by people all over the world.

Yes sir, Solomon was on the right track, but then something happened. Solomon probably continued to be intelligent, but he stopped walking in wisdom. Solomon took 700 wives and 300 concubines. Many of these marriages were as the result of treaties with other nations, but these wives, who were from a variety of cultures, brought with them a lot of false gods. Eventually, Solomon's heart was turned from the God who gave him almost literally everything. In the generation after Solomon, the nation of Israel was split in two and it was never again what it was under Solomon.

Why do I share this? Because the story of Solomon is in some ways indicative of our quest for knowledge. Why is it that so few college students graduate with their faith in tact? Some would argue that it's because when they get "enlightened," they see that faith as antiquated. Needless to say, I do not believe that is the case. Psalm 14:1 (NIV) tells us "A fool says in his heart that there is no God." How can we deny the existence of God, when the evidence of Him is all around us? I'm sorry, but the universe is far too complex to have happened by accident. Roman 1:20 reminds us "For since the creation of the world, God's invisible qualities—his eternal power and divine nature—have been clearly seen, being understood from what has been made, so that people are without excuse."(NIV) Intelligence and education are a wonderful thing. I continue to pursue mine, and you should too. We should never stop learning, but learning that separates us from God is not good.

The Beginning of Wisdom

Psalm 111:10 (NIV) says, "The fear of the Lord is the beginning of wisdom; all who follow his precepts have good understanding." If God is God, then He has all of this world figured out. He made it and and He knows how it works. He knows what works and what doesn't. True wisdom respects that, and follows what He says. God has chosen to reveal Himself through His creation and His Word. His Word is truth and any knowledge that contradicts that truth is suspect at best, diabolical at worst. To paraphrase 1 Corinthians 8:1 Knowledge sometimes puffs up, but love always builds up. The greatest knowledge is God's knowledge and the greatest love is God's love. A good and loving God has made each of us on purpose for a purpose and it is a good purpose.

I've had the privilege over the years of working with folks with special needs. For me they area tremendous joy. Some folks would look at them and focus on their lack of intellectual ability. The thing I see in them, over and over again, is their deep and abiding love for God and faith in Jesus. They may not know everything there is to know, but they know Jesus and what strikes me is, when we get to the end of our lives, that is the most important thing. In this world, the most important thing to know is not a thing, it's a person, the person of Jesus Christ. He alone is the Savior. He alone is the way to heaven. You don't know everything and the truth is you'll leave this world with questions unanswered. The most important thing to know is where you'll be when you leave this world. That answer is decided by whether or not you know Jesus. If you are smart enough to understand that, you are smart enough.

51

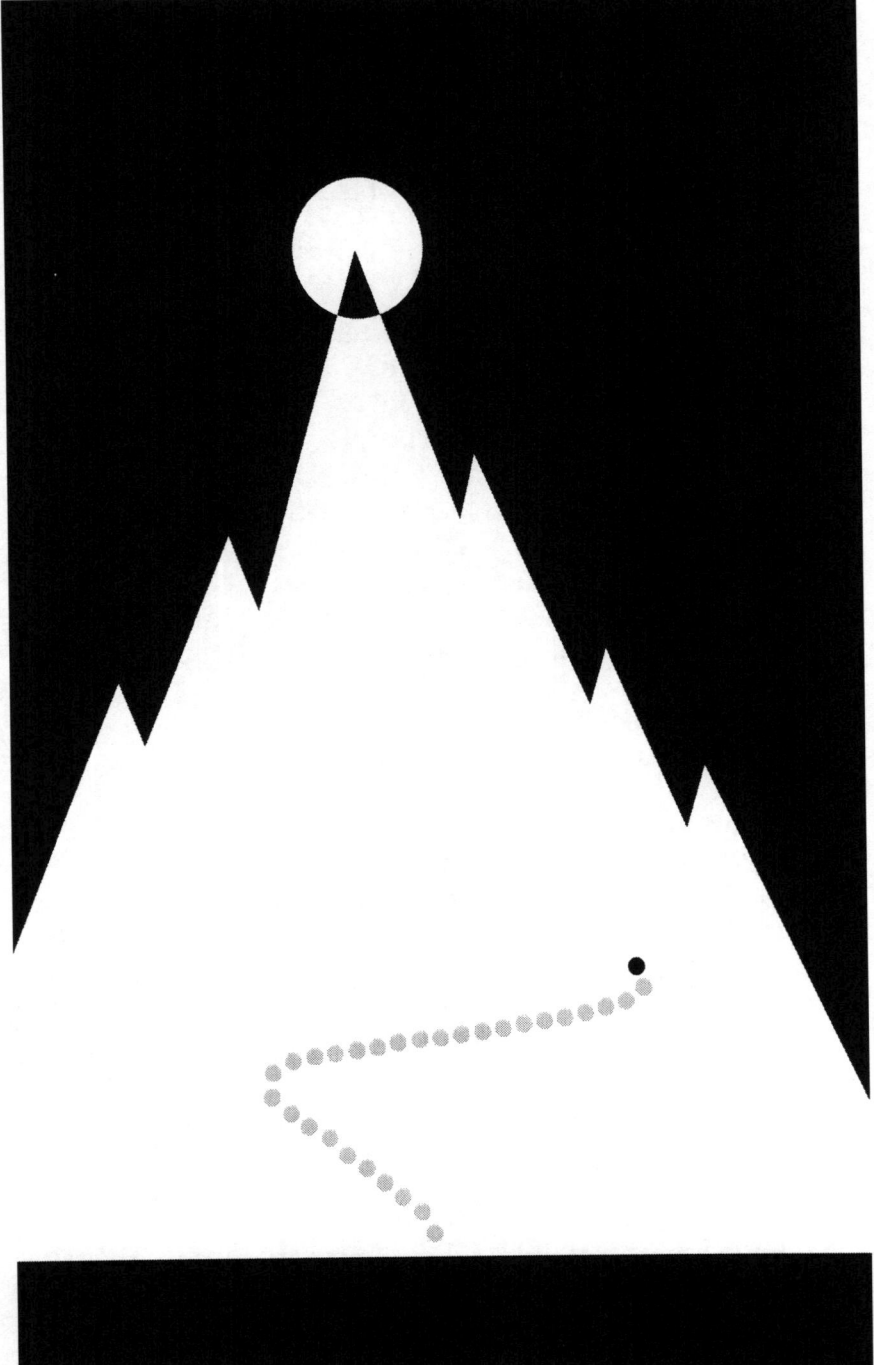

6
Made to Be Enough
God's Plan and Purpose for Our Lives

Did anyone ever tell you that you were an accident? They lied. Oh you may be the result of an unplanned pregnancy, your conception may have been in less than ideal circumstances, or you may have just been made to feel unwanted, but you are no accident. You are here on purpose and you need to know that. I'm not a fan of the theory of evolution for that very reason. It's not so much the science versus faith thing (that could be a whole book in itself and many people smarter than me have written such books) as it is the fact that it makes life seem so random and accidental and as a result, so many people exist by wandering aimlessly through this life, as if there is no real reason to be here. I'm also not a fan of the teaching of survival of the fittest. I think that line of thinking accounts for so much of the violence and anarchy in our world today, but I digress. There is a better way to think about your existence. You are enough because you were made to be enough.

You're no more accidental than the watch on your wrist or the car in your driveway. If I told you that one day your old Chevy just mutated out of the ooze, you would think I was out of my ever loving mind, yet so many people are apt to believe the exact same thing about their own existence. You need to know, you're too complex to be random. You have to be created and if you're created, then there is a Creator, and if there is a creator and you are His creation, then wouldn't you say there's a fairly good chance that there was a purpose for your creation?

One of my favorite passages of Scripture is Psalm 139(NIV). Let's look at a few verses from that passage.

Verse 1 says "You have searched me, Lord, and you know me." One of the things we know about God is that He is omniscient. More simply, this means God is all-knowing. In other words there is nothing He does not know. This includes knowing everything about us and the trajectory of our lives. The next few verses conform this:

2 You know when I sit and when I rise;
    you perceive my thoughts from afar.
3 You discern my going out and my lying down;
    you are familiar with all my ways.
4 Before a word is on my tongue
    you, Lord, know it completely.

He knows what you will do before you do it and what you will say before you say it. This is incredibly good news, It means nothing about you, or your life, surprises God. He's not up there in heaven saying, "Oh my Me, did you see what Dave Weiss just did? What am I going to do now?" We don't have to worry about all that. He has it under control. He knows it before it happens. Nothing catches Him off guard.

5 You hem me in behind and before,
    and you lay your hand upon me.
6 Such knowledge is too wonderful for me,
    too lofty for me to attain.
7 Where can I go from your Spirit?
    Where can I flee from your presence?
8 If I go up to the heavens, you are there;
    if I make my bed in the depths, you are there.
9 If I rise on the wings of the dawn,
    if I settle on the far side of the sea,
10 even there your hand will guide me,
    your right hand will hold me fast.
11 If I say, "Surely the darkness will hide me
    and the light become night around me,"

12 even the darkness will not be dark to you;
　　the night will shine like the day,
　　for darkness is as light to you.

This is more great news. God sets boundaries for us. He is always with us and there is no place we can be, where He isn't. You can't run from Him, but you will also never find yourself in a place He can't reach. We can rely on His help and guidance and there is nothing He can't see. This is incredible news about Him, but what about us? Well look at verse 13.

13 For you created my inmost being;
　　you knit me together in my mother's womb.
14 I praise you because I am fearfully and wonderfully
　　made;
　　your works are wonderful,
　　I know that full well.

Here's where the rubber meets the road. God is the Creator of everything, we'll go into this more in a later chapter but for now, what you need to see is that you are part of everything. He created you. Don't let the poetic language throw you. You are not an accidental creation. You were created by God on purpose. You're a one of a kind masterpiece. Yes I know, sometimes your mirror tells you something different. You see every flaw, ever scar, every wound and it all seems to contradict what God is saying here, but you are unique in every way, and there is a specific purpose that you are on this earth to fulfill. This is such exciting news. There is a reason for everything and there is a reason for you, right now, right the way you are. It goes on to say you are "fearfully and wonderfully made."

I've always wrestled with the "fearfully" part. Perhaps the psalmist is referring to the complexity of our make up or the awe we should have for a heavenly Father who could make something, someone, so amazing.

Wonderfully Made

Let's lock in on the second part for a moment because it is extremely important. You are "wonderfully made." That word quite literally means "full of wonder" and it's true. Think about the vast capabilities of humanity. God the creator has bestowed upon us His ability to create. We have almost limitless creative potential. We can help and serve and love and do a billion other amazing things, yet many of these things are taken for granted and we being to wonder if we're enough. Yes you are, as a matter of fact you're more than enough. You're wonderfully made and then the psalmist restates his praise for effect. "your works are wonderful, I know that full well."

My question today is do you know it? I mean really know it. Human beings baffle me sometimes, they can go to the Grand Canyon and stand in awe (and it is pretty awesome) but they can turn around and look at themselves and others and have a hard time seeing their own value. You realize, the Grand Canyon is, for all it's beauty, essentially a hole in the ground, right? If you want to see the real masterpiece, you have to look in the mirror.

The passage continues:
15 My frame was not hidden from you
    when I was made in the secret place,
    when I was woven together in the depths of the earth.

If There's a Creation, There's a Creator...

I can practically hear the science people complaining, "That's not how we're made or where we're made, that's not how any of this works." Again remember, this is poetic language, not a scientific treatise, but if you want to go there, might I suggest you think back to the book of Genesis, where Adam was formed from the dust of the earth. You might also remember that humans are made up of the same elements as is our world, so in a very real sense when we are formed in our mothers' wombs, we are, for all intents and purposes. being woven together in the depths of the earth, but again it's artistic language. That not withstanding the point is obvious, there is a design and a Designer. There is a plan and a Planner as verse 16 suggests.

> 16 Your eyes saw my unformed body;
>   all the days ordained for me were written in
>   your book before one of them came to be.

There is a Creator and you are His creation. He is omniscient, knowing everything you will ever do and every choice you will ever make. He created everything there is. Scripture reveals the plan from beginning to end and somewhere in the middle of it all is you. You are part of His plan for the universe and as such you were created and gifted to fulfill your mission, your part of the plan. If that's the case, and it is, then you have what it takes and anything you don't have, He will provide and that makes you more than enough because you were created to be enough.

What About the "Not-So-Wonderful Stuff?"

Someone reading this book might have an illness or a physical, or emotional struggle, and think I am off base in saying what I am saying. I'd like to point you to John chapter 9:1-7. In this passage, we see something really clearly, Jesus is perfect, and His disciples are not. I mean these were the guys Jesus selected to continue His work and start the Church. One of the things I love about the Bible is that it doesn't whitewash its people. Other ancient literature tends to glorify it's kings and leaders, hiding and/or omitting their flaws. The Bible, by way of contrast, shows the flaws and struggles of everyone. It even shows that the flawless, all-powerful, Jesus struggled at times with the people and their faithlessness. In John 9 we see the disciples in a particularly cringeworthy light.

Whose Fault Is It?

In their travels, they came upon a blind man, and they asked, right in front of the man, "Whose fault it was that he was blind, his or his parents?" Every time I read this, I think, "He's blind not deaf!" How could people who spent so much time in the very presence of Jesus, be this insensitive? Talk about adding insult to injury. Jesus answers their question by telling them that the fault is neither his, not his parents, "but this happened so that the works of God might be displayed in him." (John 9:3 B NIV) Of course, Jesus went on to heal the man, and gave the disciples, and others, one more reason to believe. The man had a physical struggle, not because of some sin on his or his parents' part, but so people would see the glory of God and believe. Now if you have a struggle, an illness, or anything you feel is going against you, please do not think I am making light of it in any way. Instead, I want to point you to another verse, a verse that helps us to see a light in our hardships.

Romans 8:28 (NIV) says, "And we know that in all things God works for the good of those who love him, who have been called according to his purpose." This means if we love God, He will make all things work out for our good. Yes, all things, will work out for our good. This is how we need to see hardships and especially the things that are out of our control. What if we looked for the glory in the pain? What if we looked at every situation and tried to imagine how God could be glorified in it? That would change our attitude and it would change our outlook. It would also change our witness and people would see God's glory in us. Think about it. If we could look for God's glory when we feel weak, when we don't feel like we're enough, we could still trust Him to be enough.

The Call of Jeremiah

Friend, you were made to be enough. In Jeremiah 1 we see God calling young Jeremiah to be a prophet to the nations. This would seem like an exciting call, but all Jeremiah can see is everything that's going against him. He's too young. He doesn't have the skills. The job is too big. The nation is too far fallen. It is absolutely clear that Jeremiah thinks, "There's no way I'm up to this. There's no way I'm enough." He's got all the excuses, and most of them, at least on the surface, appear to be valid. He is young and in experienced. The nation is deep in idolatry and due for judgment. They're also pretty openly hostile to the will of God. Jeremiah's excuses all look legitimate but God is just not having any of it. Why? Because Jeremiah is fearfully and wonderfully made by God and part of God's plan. God knows all of Jeremiah's strengths and weaknesses, because God made Jeremiah. He knows what's under "Jeremiah's hood." He knows what's under yours, too. I don't know what it is, but there is more to you than meets the eye. You were made on purpose for a purpose, the question is not whether or not you are enough. You were made to be enough. No the question is will you hear God's call and step into it? Will you follow God into your destiny?

In Jeremiah 1:5 (NIV) God calls to Jeremiah saying, ""Before I formed you in the womb I knew you, before you were born I set you apart; I appointed you as a prophet to the nations." Before you were born, before you were even a glisten in your mama's eye, I knew you. I set you apart. I am calling you to be a prophet.

Jeremiah's reply is telling, Verse 6 "Alas, Sovereign Lord," I said, "I do not know how to speak; I am too young." (NIV) In other words. "I'm not up to this Lord. I'm still wet behind the ears. I'm not enough." I've also noticed something about Jeremiah's excuse that you might have missed. Did you catch how Jeremiah says, "I don't know how to speak." Let me state that again, Jeremiah SAID "I don't know how to speak." He used his ability to speak to say he doesn't know how to speak. In case you think, I'm over reaching or being cute with the Scripture, please understand there is a point here. He is doing the very thing he says he doesn't have the ability to do, and too often we do the same exact thing. We are basically saying our ability is not enough, or we're not good enough or whatever other inferiorities our minds can dream up, and we need to get past that. God has given us what we need. He doesn't ask that we be better than someone else, He asks that we do our best with what He has given us. Jeremiah has the ability to speak and you have the ability to carry out your calling. God asks for faithfulness on our part, and if we will be faithful, He will take care of the rest. We need only to trust and obey because we were made to be enough.

In case you're still not convinced, look at verses 7 and 8.

But the Lord said to me, "Do not say, 'I am too young.' You must go to everyone I send you to and say whatever I command you. 8 Do not be afraid of them, for I am with you and will rescue you," declares the Lord. (NIV)

Here is the all knowing God looking at Jeremiah and essentially saying, "I know how old you are, I was there when you were born and I made you. I know the level of speaking ability you actually have, because I put that in you too. You have what you need, you're enough. What's really holding you back is fear of man. (Does that ring true in your life?) Don't be afraid? I've got you covered. In me, you're enough." And of course the biggest part of all of this is God's promise to be with us and to rescue us.

Finally God removes all the excuses and sends Jeremiah off on his mission.

9 Then the Lord reached out his hand and touched my mouth and said to me, "I have put my words in your mouth. 10 See, today I appoint you over nations and kingdoms to uproot and tear down, to destroy and overthrow, to build and to plant." (NIV)

There are no guarantees of success or accolades. Just the God's promise to be with Jeremiah through it all. The mission will be hard. One young man called as a prophet over kings and kingdoms. There will be uprooting and tearing down and you can bet that will not be popular with anyone involved, but hidden right there at the end is also a promise of restoration.

Now the good news is we have the scriptures and so we can see what happened. Jeremiah was faithful and so was God. He'll be faithful with you too. Jeremiah's life was a hard one and the thing that was holding him back was fear. I'm not sure that God ever took the fear away. Jeremiah is, after all, called the weeping prophet, and Jeremiah was given many reasons to fear. Jeremiah faced his fear, trusted the God who called him and did it anyway and that made all the difference. We can do the same. We can let God assuage our fear of not being enough and trust God to be enough. We can trust that He made us enough to do what He has called us to do.

A Masterpiece

Ephesians 2:10 says that we are God's workmanship. Consider all that He has made and yet He made humanity last and best. If you are His workmanship, you are a masterpiece. People say God can do anything and everything and that is not entirely true. There are a few things that are outside his nature. For example, God cannot fail. Everything He makes works by His perfect design and He made you. The rest of the verse says we were created in Christ Jesus. We were created in and by our perfect Savior, and we were created to do good works, which God prepared in advance for us to do. He created you individually, on purpose for a purpose. That purpose is a big part of the meaning of you life. He equipped you to do something good in this world, and He put in you what you need to do what He has called you to do.

You might see a flaw in what I just said, "I feel called to do "x" but I don't have this thing, trait or quality that I need to get it done." That may be true, but did you notice the verse is plural. His plan is not for us alone. We were also created to be in community. God will put into your life the components you are lacking. through people, new gifts or a multitude of other ways. Our duty today is to take the next right step, trusting that God made you to be enough and that He is more than enough.

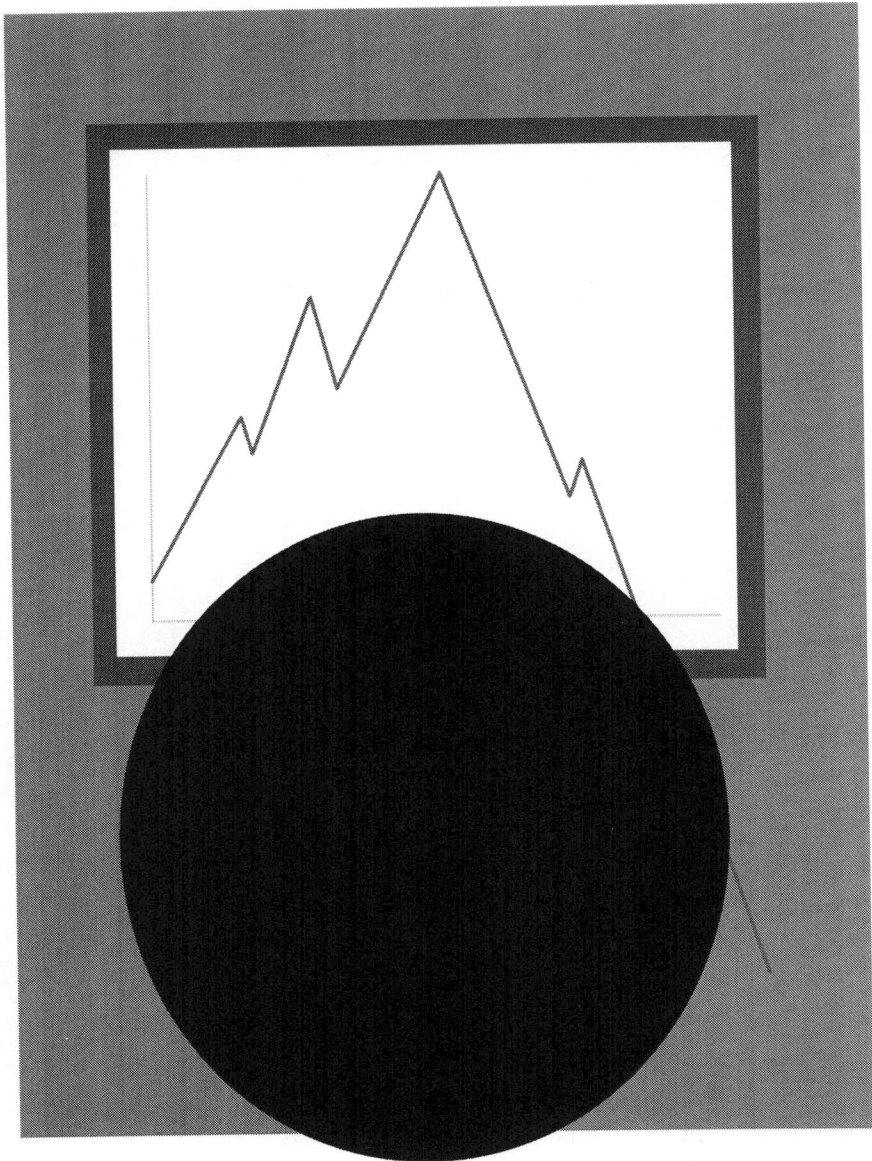

7
Am I Doing Enough?
Workaholism and the Need to Achieve

I think I need to start this chapter off with a confession, or maybe better stated an admission.

Hi, my names is Dave W. and I am a workaholic.

It seems to come naturally to me. I tend toward excess in every area of life. People think I don't drink because I'm a pastor, maybe even that I might be judgmental. That's not the case. Oh, I do want to set a good example, and I never would want to lead anyone astray. I know that the Scripture says people in my position will be judged more harshly, and I know that to be true, at least when it comes to the opinions of men, but those are not the primary reasons. The primary reason is when I did drink, I drank to excess, nearly every single time. When I start something, I have a hard time finding the "off switch." Now for the record, I believe I have been set free from alcohol, but I'm not sure I believe it enough to test the hypothesis, so instead, I don't drink. I quit and with God's help, I will never go back. There are some things you can't quit cold turkey though, and one of those is working.

I have a great dad. He took a lot of pride in providing for our family. He took even more pride that my mom could be a stay-at-home mom. As a result, he worked two jobs for much of my childhood. I don't hold that against him, I admired it. I admired it so much that I have had at least two jobs for much of my adult life, but there was a problem. No matter how hard I tried. I never quite felt like I measured up. My wife still had to work and try as I might I never felt like I succeeded. I worked a full time job, often had a part time job and I also did all the freelance art work I could get my hands on. If I didn't have enough of that, I would work on spec, creating original art and sending it out to companies to see if they would buy it or commission me to do something for them, as the case may be. I was working all the time, but it didn't seem to matter. I just couldn't get ahead.

My mantra was always the same, "If I just work harder, I'll get there." The thing is, "there" was a moving target. I used to drive my wife crazy. Any time I saw anybody, but especially my dad, I would rattle off a list of all the things I was doing. It was all I wanted to talk about. In truth I wanted him to be impressed with me. I wanted him to be proud of me. The thing is, I know today that he was probably already proud of me. The problem was I wasn't proud of me. I was already a Christian by this time, and I would have proudly told you so, but my identity wasn't in Christ. My identity was in my work. I'm betting yours might be, too.

What You Are and What You Do

You want to know how I know. If I were to walk up to you in a crowd and ask "Who are you?" How long would it take before you told me about your job? Oh don't be upset. If you didn't tell me, I'd probably ask. It's something we want to know about each other. It's not a problem to be proud of what you do, well unless you become prideful, but let's assume that's not the case, at least for now. The problem comes when you can't separate what you do from who you are. That was my issue. I took such great pride in being an artist, that nothing else was good enough and it had to be the right kind of art. My first art job was designing circulars for a grocery store chain. When I first got the job, I was happy, because at least I could say I was a "professional artist" i.e. I got paid to make art. It didn't take long though to realize that work wasn't fulfilling. Why? Because when I told people I was an artist, they would say things like, "Oh cool, so what do you do, watercolor? oils?" and I would have to say, "no... groceries." At which point I always felt like they gave me looks of pity. My identity was so tied up in what I did, that I couldn't just enjoy where I was and appreciate the doors that were opened. Groceries allowed me to buy groceries but I wanted more.

Now to be clear, there is nothing wrong with wanting to grow in your career and there is nothing wrong with wanting to broaden your horizons. You may not be where you want to be. That's okay, keep trying and do what it takes, but whatever you do, do not get your identity from what you do. If you're a believer, what you do is not your identity. Your identity, first and foremost, is that you are a child of God. Who you are is not what you do.

I was highly dissatisfied with life and that made my family feel terrible. I wasn't happy because, in my own mind, I wasn't enough. They looked at my lack of happiness and it made them wonder if they weren't enough. It wasn't about them. I loved them. They were the best thing in my life, but I looked at what I could do for them and I never felt like enough. It wasn't about them, the problem was with me, but I was becoming their problem. I was deceived into believing that if I just worked a little harder, I'd become what I was supposed to be. I'd become enough. It never worked.

The reason why was simple. I was already enough. God had made me enough. He proved it to me by rescuing me at the price of His Son. If you are a believer, He has done the same for you. The God of the universe loves you, and likely so do a lot of other people. You don't have to do enough to be enough, Christ did all the doing and He made you enough.

The other side of getting your identity from what you do is discouragement. I've had a few jobs over the years where it felt like no matter what I did, nothing was ever going to be good enough. Whether that is true or not, remains to be seen, but that is how it felt. I could have great work going out over and over again and it always seemed like no one noticed, but let there be a mistake and it was as if the world fell apart. Now to be clear, some of this was the job, but most of it was me. I was still getting my identity from what I did, so when there was a mistake, it began to feel like I was a mistake. As a result, I became extremely discouraged. Mistakes stopped being mistakes and started to mean, at least in my heart and mind, that I was a failure, a loser, you name it. Eventually I just started to give up. When that happened, no one was happy and God was not glorified in my life. You simply cannot afford to get your identity tied up in what you do.

I mentioned earlier about the way I would always feel like I had to tell my dad all the things that I was doing in hopes that he would be proud of me. Well I was assigning those same attributes to God. I thought if I did enough, God would be proud of me, and for a while I carried that into the ministry. Surely if I did enough, God would bless my efforts and make things happen. That's not how this works. What God desires from us is not success, but faithfulness and faithfulness is not found in some workaholic drive to succeed. Faithfulness is found in doing the best you can with what you have and trusting God in any area where you find yourself lacking. What I was trying to do was earn God's love and prove myself worthy of Salvation. Neither of those things is possible and, don't miss this, neither of those things is necessary, God doesn't love us based on some scale of accomplishment. It's not like He's saying "Do more and I'll love you more, Do less and I'll love you less." No, His love is perfect. He couldn't love us any more, because His love is complete and He wouldn't love us any less, because that would be less than perfect.

Likewise, I couldn't make myself worthy of salvation by my own efforts, because if I could, Jesus wouldn't have had to die. All have sinned and fallen short of the glory of God. We sinned so He died. Are you feeling any freedom yet? Ephesians 2:8,9 (NIV) says, "For it is by grace that you have been saved, through faith—and this is not from yourselves, it is the gift of God—not by works so that no one can boast." The key element here is by grace. Grace is undeserved, unmerited favor. You can't earn it, you couldn't deserve it, but God gave it, not because you're good, but because He is good. When it comes to salvation, we don't need to work harder to receive it, we just have to believe it, through faith in the finished work of Jesus Christ on the cross. It's not from ourselves, it's a gift. And then he restates, it's never received by works so that we can't boast about it. The only thing we can really boast about, is not a thing, it's a person, our Savior Jesus.

Faith and Deeds

Does this mean there is nothing for us to do? Absolutely not. You are in this world on a mission to glorify God. Faith is manifested in deeds. James writes: "What good is it, my brothers and sisters, if someone claims to have faith but has no deeds? Can such faith save them?" (James 2:14 NIV) This also sounds like we're going back to earning salvation doesn't it? Well it isn't. Our works are not about earning, they're about appreciation and obedience, We serve God and others out of appreciation for what He has done for us in Christ, so that others might see, and come to believe. That is what it means to serve to the glory of God.

We are gifted to glorify. James goes on to write "Suppose a brother or a sister is without clothes and daily food. If one of you says to them, "Go in peace; keep warm and well fed," but does nothing about their physical needs, what good is it?" (James 2:15-16 NIV) In other words, if we see a need we are supposed to try to meet it. One of the things I like to say is if you see a situation in our world and it puts a burden on your heart to the point where you say "Someone should do something about that." you should probably realize that someone just might be you.

James goes on to say, "In the same way, faith by itself, if it is not accompanied by action, is dead." (James 2:17 NIV) Our works show our faith, or put a different way, our faithfulness shows up as faith in action. Again this is not about earning, it's about obedience and appreciation and just plain doing what's right. In this world there is plenty of "right" to be done, but we are still not to define ourselves by what we do. Our identity has to be in Christ alone, otherwise, our work might very well become an idol in our lives.

Every time I would see my dad, I would boast. I wanted him to be proud of me but he was already proud of me, so all my efforts to make him proud were in vain. I was trying to earn what I already had. That's ridiculous. Now my dad is a great guy, but he's not perfect. If my dad can get it right, don't you think the Creator of the universe can? You already have God's love, no need to earn it, it's yours and if you believe in Jesus, if He is your Lord and Savior, you already have salvation, no need to earn that either. And by the way, if you don't know if you have it, Salvation is yours for the asking. Place your trust in Jesus, believe that what He did on the cross, He did for you, and ask Him to be your Lord and Savior and He will. The good news is, He really wants you to do that. It may even be the reason He led me to write this book. He is good and He loves you already. No need to earn it, no need to prove yourself, just turn from the stuff that you know is messing up your life, and ask Him to forgive you. Accept and believe.

You Deserve a Break Today...

There is one last thing we need to cover here and that is the topic of rest. If you ever find yourself feeling guilty for taking a break, chances are awfully good that your priorities are out of whack. If you think everything will stop unless you keep going, you are desperately out of balance. Remember all the way back in Exodus, when God gave us the Ten Commandments? Do you remember the one where He said "Remember the Sabbath day by keeping it holy. Six days you shall labor and do all your work, but the seventh day is a sabbath to the Lord your God. On it you shall not do any work..." (Exodus 20:8-10A NIV) God did that on purpose. If you go further into the law you will see that the penalty for breaking the Sabbath in the Old Testament was death. Sounds like God takes Sabbath pretty seriously.

Now I don't want to dwell on the legalism of the Sabbath. Jesus fought that enough in His earthly life and ministry. Jesus proved He was Lord of the Sabbath and more importantly that the Sabbath was made for man and not man for the Sabbath. That last part is key. The Sabbath was made for you and me. A day of rest was planned into the order of the universe from week one, because the God who made us, knew we needed it. A good deal of Sabbath has to do with worship, but there is something more. Put very simply, it's love. The God of the universe knew that if we were not ordered to take time off, we would find a way to fill every minute of our time. We would start to put other things in front of Him, destroy our relationship with Himself and work ourselves into an early grave. That is not at all what God desires for us.

The thing we all need to remember, in our quest to be enough, by doing enough and working enough, is that God is already enough and we can depend on Him in every aspect of our lives, This is huge and crucial. It means that it doesn't all depend on us and that we can trust Him to keep going what needs to keep going while we give our bodies, as well as our minds and souls the rest that they need to function in God's world.

You are not what you do. Should you bring your best to what you do? Of course! The Bible tells us in 1 Corinthians 10:31 (NIV) to do everything we do to the glory of God. Colossians 3:23 (NIV) takes it even further. "Whatever you do, work at it with all your heart, as working for the Lord, not for human masters." In the next verse Paul goes so far as to tell us why "since you know that you will receive an inheritance from the Lord as a reward. It is the Lord Christ you are serving." (1 Corinthians 10:32 NIV) That's faithfulness. We serve as if we are serving God and for good reason. When we serve, that is precisely who we are ultimately supposed to be serving. We are either serving Him directly or we are serving Him by being a blessing to those He loves. We need to bring our best to everything, but remember God doesn't need you. There is nothing you can do that God can't do a million, billion times better all by Himself, but that's not the point. No, God desires you. He desires to be with you, for you to work by His side, and on His mission. You're His beloved child. Work in Him and rest in Him.

If you're being faithful, you're doing enough.

8
Enough is Enough!
Coming to the End of Self

He was a very famous man. If you have ever watched the news in the U.S., you would know his name. He's an advisor to world leaders and when he speaks, the world pays attention, and they have for decades. I was thrilled to find out he was a man of faith and even more excited when I found out he was speaking at my friend and mentor's church. I was so excited to hear what he had to say. This was a man whose name is synonymous with excellence in his field, and I fully expected a message laced with stories from his work. While the message was peppered with a few anecdotes from that phase of his life, the message took a decidedly different turn.

He began to speak of addiction and alcoholism and his battle with the bottle. I knew nothing of this part of his life, most of the world probably doesn't, which is why I have not shared his name. Ultimately this was a story of triumph and victory in Jesus, but in the midst of it all, he made a statement I will not likely ever forget. He said, "Rock bottom is a holy place, because when you hit it, the only thing you can do is look up." I thought that statement was one of the most profound things I have ever heard, and I could relate, because I had hit rock bottom, too.

One night, when I was drunk and suicidal for the umpteenth time, right in the midst of trying to end it all, I had a revelation. I didn't want to die, I just couldn't keep living the way I was living one more day, and so instead of taking my life, I cried out in prayer to a God I wasn't sure I believed in and a God I didn't know at all. It was the simplest of prayers, the three word prayer of a desperate man, "God help me" and there at the place we call rock bottom, God reached down and began the process that would rescue me forever. Please understand if you are reading this book, the reason it exists is precisely because when I cried out to God for help, He helped me.

Rock bottom was my holy place, too. I looked up and was radically transformed forever. It was after that day at bottom that most of the best things in my life happened, my marriage, my kids, my grandson and this adventure called ministry that has taken me to amazing places and allowed me to do extraordinary things. I almost missed it all. It's for that reason I call this season my bonus life. In that moment of crying out to God from the bottom of a deep pit, it was as if I said "enough's enough."

You Don't Have to Hit Bottom

Have you been there? Have you been to a place where you know you've hit bottom and you have no choice but to look up? It's okay if you haven't. You don't need to go there and there is no honor in the plunge. You can call out to God long before you hit bottom. Smart people don't have to fall that far, they see a need, and they go to God. They see the trajectory of the path they are on and they make a turn. By the way, that turn is called repentance and it is available to us all at any time.

I have to laugh sometimes because it seems there are two schools of though on this whole rock bottom thing. Not long after I got my call to ministry and began my training, there was at least one person who commented, "And to think, they're going to let him be a minister after all he has done." The thing is if past sin disqualifies someone from ministry, only one was ever qualified and we nailed Him to a cross for His troubles. "All have sinned and fallen short of the glory of God." If we disqualify the repentant, there is no one left, except the unrepentant and they really are disqualified.

The other side of this coin is the disdain some people seem to have for people who haven't even been to rock bottom. Some people see a bloody testimony as the only real qualification for ministry. They see people who have grown up in the church as something less than those of us who have bottomed out. God forbid. I have a bloody, messy testimony, but I raised my kids to have a safe "bottom free" testimony. I raised them to love God without all the stupid choices it took me to get there. They are no less saved than I am and I think this is a huge point. I looked at my cycle of sin and thought "Enough's enough." As much as I am able to determine it, this ends here in my generation. I have good parents. My failure is my own, but with God's help it stops here. Let my sons start a new, blessed generation, as children of a man who loves God. The thing we need to remember is, everyone has been rescued. Some have to be pulled from a pit, while others are rescued by being raised to know Christ from their earliest days. Both groups need Jesus, and when they come to Jesus, both groups are saved.

Before I go any further, I need to make a statement. The famous man I wrote of in the beginning was almost entirely, but not quite completely, correct in his statement that rock bottom is a holy place. Most people do hit bottom and look up but occasionally you run into another type of person. They hit rock bottom and try to dig their way out. These people need to learn a very valuable lesson. You cannot dig your way out of a hole. In some cases, this comes from things like addiction. In others it's a pridefully misguided self-reliance. Still others seem to be happy to wallow in the hole they've dug for themselves or they just give up hope of things being any better. If you've ever found yourself in this place or maybe even find yourself there right now. There is something you need to know. When you're at bottom, the way out is always up and there's a better than even chance you can't make that climb alone. Pray and ask God for help.

A Prodigal Parable

Jesus told a parable of a man who hit bottom. He had everything going for him, but greed and pride pushed him over the edge. His story is found in Luke 15. While this is not a true story, but rather an illustration, it shares a great truth that resonates with many people.

There was a rather wealthy man, a farmer, who had two sons. The older son was a hard working man. He has problems of his own and he is actually the main reason Jesus told the story, but for now our main focus is on the younger brother. One day the younger brother had enough of the hard work of farm life. He thought "Dad has tons of money. I could live well for years without all this hard work if I could just get my inheritance now." So he went to His father and asked for just that.

Now let's freeze the story there for a second. Do you realize how harsh, cold and thoughtless this is? By asking his father for his inheritance in advance, he is essentially saying to his father, "I can't wait until you die. I want it all and I want it now!" Can you imagine the devastation you would feel if someone you love did this to you? Now again we need to remember, this is not a true story, it's an illustration. The father in the story represents God and the sons represent us. The younger son asking for the advance inheritance is essentially the same as when we go to God expecting His blessings but not living to honor him. This is the essence of sin.

Back to our story. Most of us would probably have responded differently, but the father hears his son's request and grants it. Now according to Jewish law, the older son would have received a double share, so essentially the younger son would receive a third of the estate. He just received a third of everything the father worked his entire life to gain. Suddenly the younger son finds himself with a fat wallet and few responsibilities. The very next day he took off to a far country, and like many young men who end up with money rapidly, so begins the party. At first it's great. He's living that old Styx song, You know, "[He's] got dozens of friends and the fun never ends, that is as long as [he's] buying." And that's how it goes until one day, his first century equivalent of a credit card is declined. Once that happens it's a different story. All his "friends in low places" are gone, and he find himself alone, broke and lonely, not to mention homeless. His inheritance is gone and he finds himself in dire need.

As Jesus tells it, he is so desperate that he hires himself out to a farmer in that country, feeding hogs, He's so hungry that he wants to eat the pig slop, but his employers won't even let him have that. It's time to freeze the story again. We may not get the significance of this as 21st century people. We think that being a pig farmer isn't so bad. I like bacon, how about you? The reason we may not see the problem is we are not first century Jewish people. Jesus tells the story this way because He is trying to show us a man who hit rock bottom. This man was so desperate that he was feeding hogs. This means he was working for gentiles, since only gentiles would have pigs. Jewish people of that time did not associate with gentiles. Jesus was about to fix that but his disgruntled First Century Jewish audience would not have been prepared for that just yet. Secondly, the fact that he was feeding pigs would have been worst. Pigs were seen as unclean animals to the Jewish people. To even touch a pig could make a Jewish person ritually unclean, unable to enter the temple and, by extension, the presence of God. By crafting His story in such a way as to have this character feeding pigs, Jesus is show-ing us a man that has hit rock bottom. In case anyone missed that point, Jesus took it further by showing that the man was willing to eat the pig slop, but he was deprived of it. That's desperation.

The younger son, who we call the prodigal, was at bottom and it was at bottom that he looked up. He began to think that his father's servants had all the food that they wanted, while he starved. He realized, in his heart, that he was probably no longer worthy to be called a son, but maybe his father would have mercy and take him on as a hired hand. He may have blown his inheritance, but maybe there was a chance at survival. With that thought in mind, he headed for home.

The whole way home, he rehearsed his speech. "Father, I have sinned against heaven and against you. I am no longer worthy to be called your son; make me like one of your hired servants." (Luke 15:18-19 NIV) That was what he was planned to say, but when he was still a long way off, he saw someone coming toward him. It was his father and he was running. Some scholars say this represents another point that Jesus was trying to make. They say that running for Jewish men of standing was seen as very undignified. If this is the case, Jesus is showing us a father who is so happy he is willing to leave his dignity behind. He's not trying to figure out how to deal with his son or whether or not he would receive him, he's been looking, and waiting, and hoping, for his son to return and when he returns, the father abandons all social convention and runs to his son.

The son is still unsure. Jesus, in his story, even has him begin the speech. "'Father, I have sinned against heaven and against you. I am no longer worthy to be called your son." (Luke 15:21) but also note, the father never lets the son finish his speech. He's too busy shouting orders to listen. No, he's not shouting orders at the son, as some of us might have been tempted to do. He's shouting to his servants. "Quick! Bring the best robe and put it on him. Put a ring on his finger and sandals on his feet. Bring the fattened calf and kill it. Let's have a feast and celebrate. For this son of mine was dead and is alive again; he was lost and is found." So they began to celebrate.(Luke 15:22-24 NIV) He's redressing the son. no shabby, pig encrusted robes for his child. And shoes, make sure he has new shoes that haven't been sullied by the mess of the sty, but the really big thing is the ring on his finger. The meaning of this is simple. He will never be his father's hired man. The father is reinstating him as a son. They kill the fattened calf. Usually they were fattened for a sacrifice. The father is praising God for the return of his son.

Remember once again, this is a parable. It's a simple story Jesus used to help believers understand something complicated. The dead is alive. The lost is found. The child is reinstated. Make no mistake about it, Jesus is saying when you come to the end of yourself, when you hit bottom. when it's finally time to say enough's enough, all you have to do is turn around and come home. The father will be right there to receive you and reinstate you to your position as His child. It's called repentance and repentance is always followed by grace and forgiveness.

That is at least from God.

The Older Brother

It's always important to remember as we look at parables, we need to look at the original audience because this gives the motivation for the parable. The themes of grace and forgiveness are there and for us all, but the original audience for this parable were people who were having a hard time showing grace and forgiveness. While most of us are represented by the prodigal, Jesus was speaking to people who were acting like the older brother. Remember the prodigal comes home and the father lavishes love upon him, kills the fatted calf and throws a party. We're not sure where the older brother was when all that was going on, but most likely he was out with his nose to the proverbial grindstone, getting all the work done and taking up the slack left behind by his younger brother. When he hears the sound of music and finds out the source of the festivities is the return of his prodigal brother, he is irate. When the father comes in to invite him into the party, he refuses the invitation. He simply cannot accept that his brother could be forgiven. Many of us have similar difficulties.

We have been serving faithfully for so long that we tend to forget that we too have been prodigal and in need of forgiveness. This is a truth we all need to hold close to our hearts. The forgiven need to forgive and recipients of grace must freely dispense grace.

Who Are You In This Story?

As I look at the story, one of the things I have come to realize is that each of us have, at one point or another, been each of the characters in this story. We've all been prodigal, maybe not to the extent of the younger son, but we have all received the blessings of God and chosen to go another way, rather than His way. We've also all been like the father and yes, I know you're tempted to kick against that. You'll want to say to me, "No Dave, the father in the story is God and I'm not that good." I'll give you that, but I bet you love someone who is going in the direction of the prodigal. There is most likely someone in your life who you hope will turn from what they're doing and come back home. Trust me when I tell you, your heavenly Father loves that person even more than you do, so keep praying, and live in the expectation that God will come through. Then be ready to run.

Finally most of us struggle with older brother feelings against someone and we need to remember that we have received grace, mercy and forgiveness and what we have freely received, we also need to freely give.

So where are you today? Are you at rock bottom today? If you are, put down the shovel and look up. When you find yourself in a pit, help always comes from above. If you're struggling with unforgiveness, remember the grace you have received and live accordingly. Jesus commanded us to forgive as we've been forgiven. Here's what that means, if you're not forgiving, you're in your own place of prodigal-ness. Maybe today is the day to look at your propensity to be prodigal and say "Enough's enough." Your father is ready to receive you. Turn around, run into His arms and receive a blessing that is more than enough.

9

When You've Had Enough
Exploring and Extending Grace and Forgiveness

Some of the toughest things to navigate in this world are relationships. Oh, when they're great, they're great, but what do you do when people become antagonistic, when they're working on your last nerve, when you've just plain had enough?

Well the short answer is grace and forgiveness, but this topic is not easy enough for short answers, so let's dig in a little bit more by looking at three different kinds of relationships: church relationships, family relationships and other relationships.

I'd like to start with church relationships. The reason for that is simple, church relationships, provided everyone is a believer, are eternal relationships. They should last well beyond this world. Jesus said something to the effect of "where two or three are gathered, I am there in their midst." This verse is, I think often misused, but we'll get to that in a bit. There's something else that I'm pretty sure Jesus knew about people and that is "where two are three are gathered, there will likely be four or more opinions." I made that last part up, but I'm sure if that occurred to me, the Creator of the Universe surely already knew it. As a matter of fact, I'm sure He knew, because in Matthew 18, Jesus gave us a way to deal with the conflict all those diverse opinions will assuredly bring, sooner or later—even between believers.

Crushing Conflict Jesus' Way

The first thing I would like you to notice is that this passage is exclusively for the church. I know this because the passage begins with "If your brother or sister sins against you…" We'll see further evidence of this going forward, but this passage is for the family of God, the Church. Again this is largely because these are eternal relationships, but beyond that, the church is supposed to be a "place" (the church is the people) of unity, where people work to restore relationships. It was never designed to be a place of turmoil. This is, at least in part, because a primary reason the church exists is to attract unbelievers to the faith and to the Lord and why should they come into a church that's full of turmoil, especially if they can find less turmoil some place else? The other reason for this is because we serve a God who is all about relationships. He created us for the purpose of being in relationship with us, to love us and for us to love him. Even before He created us, His trinitarian nature, as Father, Son and Holy Spirit shows us that He is, in a sense, a relationship unto Himself. Yes, God is all about relationships and His chief goal in everything is to restore relationships, both between Him and us (which is why Jesus came), as well as our human relationships, especially within the Body of Christ.

So again Jesus tells us that if a brother or sister sins against us, we're supposed to go in loaded for bear, having built an army around our side of the argument, so we can crush the erring spiritual sibling and win the fight, right? No! We're supposed to go to them, just between the two of us. We're supposed to have a conversation, talk it out, work it out, get it out in the open, early and get it solved before the whole thing festers or blows up. And you know it would work, right? A simple discussion, right at the onset, is usually enough to work things out. Easy peasy! So why don't we do it? Well probably because we think they won't listen.

The omniscient (all-knowing) Jesus already knew this would be our objection, so he answers it. If they won't listen, "...take one or two others along, so that 'every matter may be established by the testimony of two or three witnesses." (Matthew 18:16 NIV) You know what this is all about, right? If the other person won't listen, take someone along, a neutral party, someone who is a little bit more calm, cool and collected to be a sort of mediator. Again the purpose of this action is to restore the relationship, and it would work, you know it would. So why don't we do it? Well this time, I think the answer is two-fold. The first part is pride. What if you go to all the trouble of bringing in this third party mediator and he or she hears both sides of the story. Now you are thoroughly convinced they will find in favor of you, but what if he or she hears both sides of the story, looks at you and says, "Sorry buddy, you're the problem." That's one possibility, the other is the same as before, a constant objection that stands in the way of so many reconciliations, "What if they won't listen?"

Once again Jesus proves his omniscience and answers the question before we even ask it. "If they still refuse to listen, tell it to the church…" (Matthew 18:17a NIV) Now this brings up a larger issue, what does it mean to tell it to the church? Does it mean that when it comes to the time in your worship service for the "sharing of joys and concerns" that you unload it before the whole body? "You're not going to believe what so and so did to me…" Yeah, probably not. No, what this means is you take your dispute to the leadership of the church and allow them to mediate the situation for the purpose of restoring the relationship. This is the other reason I say this passage is only really for the church. Suppose your dispute is with your unbelieving neighbor. What are you going to do? Go to them and say, "You need to come to my church so my church leaders can mediate this." I don't think so. First of all, they're not going to come. Secondly, even if they do, they will not submit to the authority of your church leaders, because your church leaders have no authority with them. No, if you try this with an unbelieving neighbor and they actually agree to go, chances you should just apologize right away, because they are so convinced that you're wrong that they know you're going to look stupid in front of your whole church leadership and they want to be there to see it.

So again, this is for believers, and if both parties to the dispute are committed believers, under the authority of the local church, this process should work well. The offended parties should submit to the findings of those in authority over them and the relationship should be quickly restored. Even if nothing else was going to work, this should work. So why don't we do it? Well maybe pride is a factor. We don't really want our church leadership to know we have problems. As a church leader, I can tell you, if it gets to this level, they already know, but the second reason is the same as it has been every time, "What if they won't listen?"

By now it should surprise no one when I say Jesus already knew the objection was coming, so he answered it once again. "and if they refuse to listen even to the church, treat them as you would a pagan or a tax collector." (Matthew 18:17b NIV) About this time I can practically hear your collective sighs of relief, dear readers. You're thinking, "If it gets to the church and they still won't listen, I can be done with them, right? I can wash my hands of them now, right? They're dead to me, that's what you're saying, right?" Well you seem a little to eager, so lets examine this. Jesus said to treat them like a "pagan or a tax collector," right? Now the pagan thing is easy. The pagan of Jesus' day and age would be anyone who was not a follower of the God of Israel. In first century Israel, that would have been the Gentiles. Jesus' predominantly Jewish audience didn't associate with Gentiles at that time so some might assume that would be a signal to write them off, but lets go further. Why does he call out the tax collectors? Well if you go back to an earlier chapter where we discussed the tax collectors, you know they were hated, corrupt, turncoats and outcasts. You might assume this was another signal to write off our offenders. No so fast.

Who wrote the book of Matthew? I know there are some experts who debate this point, but for the most part, the church widely agrees that the book of Matthew was written by Matthew. Do you know what Matthew was doing for a living when Jesus called him to be a disciple? That's right, Matthew was a tax collector. Now let's revisit the pagan part of the quote. Who spoke this passage? This passage was spoken by none other than Jesus Christ. Anyone remember what Jesus did for pagans? That's right he stretched out his arms and died for them. Does it sound like Matthew, the former tax collector would tell us to write off the tax collectors? I seriously doubt it. After all Jesus didn't write Matthew off and do you honestly think that Jesus who died for the pagans would tell us to write off the pagans? Since it's His will that none should perish but all come to repentance, I'm going to guess that's a no as well. What I think Jesus is saying is if someone who claims to be a believer will not work to restore a relationship, or come under the authority of the local church, their status as a believer is in question. As such, like pagans and the corrupt tax collectors, they are not to be written off, but perhaps we ought to consider that they are still part of the mission field. We still love them. We don't give up. We simply redouble our efforts in different ways. Maybe at this point the tensions are pretty high and we need to distance ourselves for a while, but we still pray and look for the opportunity to do our part to make things right.

As a little aside, Jesus doesn't end the teaching there. He goes on to say. "Truly I tell you, whatever you bind on earth will be bound in heaven, and whatever you loose on earth will be loosed in heaven. (Matthew 18:18 NIV) These verses in some ways don't seem to go with the teaching above or the story below, but they do, as a matter of fact, they are crucial, especially in response to the "take it to the church" aspect of conflict resolution. Similar to understanding a parable, part of the importance of this teaching is knowing who is receivin g it. This is revealed in the first verse of the chapter. Jesus' disciples came to him with a question and He began to teach them. Keep in mind who these disciples would become. They would be the first leaders of a new church, the Church of Jesus Christ and in verse 18 he is telling something of the authority, and with that the responsibility, they would be given as leaders. He is telling them that they would have the authority over important decisions and in a sense people's lives through their teaching. Think about the importance of this. Jesus' primary persecutors, through most of His ministry, were the people who should have loved Him most, the religious leaders. Jesus wants something better from those He places in authority. In this verse Jesus is showing the leaders of the coming church how to deal with the things that are brought before them.

It's for this reason that the next verse can be said, "Again, truly I tell you that if two of you on earth agree about anything they ask for, it will be done for them by my Father in heaven." (Matthew 18:19 NIV) Now this is not meaning they can just go asking for things willy-nilly. This is not the "golden ticket, ask for the mansion and yacht" thing some people treat it as. At another place Jesus adds the caveat that we ask in His name. This is the key. We're not asking for just anything. We're asking for what He would ask for, guided by His spirit. To ask in His name is to make a request on His behalf. These are the requests the Father will grant.

I HATE Onions

I've tried for some time to come up with a way to make this clear and I think I've got it. I hate onions. I can't stand them, the flavor, the texture, to me they're repulsive. Now suppose I asked you to get me something for lunch, and you decide you're going to try to fix my aversion to onions, (others have tried. All have failed.) so you go out and order me an onion sandwich, french onion soup, a side of onion rings and something onion flavored to drink. If you were to do that, I hope you're hungry, because I ain't eating it. Your ordered something for me, but you definitely did not order in my name. If we expect God to deliver on this promise. We need to be seeking Him together, and looking for what He would ask for,

Two or More

And then we get to verse 20, "For where two or three gather in my name, there am I with them." There are a lot of verses in the Bible that get misused, out of context. This one is probably the most well meaning. I remember when I was pastoring a church plant. There were a couple times when our numbers were pretty sparse. Once or twice there were only four people in the room and at least two of them beside me, were named Weiss. I tried to hide my disappointment, but I wasn't overly good at it and someone would come up to me with this verse as a way to comfort me. To be clear, I loved them for it, but that's not what this verse means. How do I know? Because I'm a born again believer in Jesus Christ and when I came to Christ, He gave His Spirit to live in me. The Holy Spirit is the third part of the trinity, so by definition, He is God, therefore I need no one else for God to be in my "midst." If I am somewhere, even if I'm all by myself, God is there, by virtue of God's promise and that same promise applies to every believer. This verse is about leadership. This is about leaders gathering together to make the complex decisions that church leaders sometimes have to make, and assuring us that if we will gather in His name, seeking what He would ask for, He will be there with them and guide them to the right decisions. Again the reason for this is because relationships in the church are hugely important and it is vital that we seek His wisdom to make all of our decisions. The world is watching what we do and so conflicts must be resolved.

Is There a Time to Give Up?

Before we move on to family relationships, I need to say something about the most difficult part of all of this. By the way, this is for all relationships. Is there ever a time when reconciling a relationship is a bad idea? The answer is a qualified yes. None of what we have been saying up to this point is meant to put anyone in danger. You were not created to be a victim of violence, abuse, etc. Staying in a relationship with someone doing you harm, especially physical harm, is not a good idea. Sometimes you have to look at a situation and say, "Enough!" It's not wrong to notify the authorities and/or to get yourself out of a bad situation. Forgiveness is biblically mandated (We'll get to this more in a moment.) being a victim is not. So as we move into the rest of this chapter keep that in mind.

Family Relationships

There's that old saying, "You always hurt the one you love." Now again if you're reading this and you're being physically harmed, go back to the previous paragraph. I'm not talking about violence here, I'm talking about the stuff that happens in normal relationships. The truth in that old saying is obvious. The relationships we care the most about are with the people closest to us. These people are part of our hearts and, as a result, disputes with them are the hardest to endure and hurt the most. That being said, the family is the essential building block of society and God designed it to be all that and more. For the most part, we can't just look at family and say "Enough." We need to find ways to reconcile the relationship. Fortunately God gave us plenty of guidelines in His Word to show us how to do that very thing or even better, to avoid having anything to reconcile.

Marriage

The basic building block of the culture and the basic building block of the family is the marriage. Strong marriages are essential to society and to God's plan for the world. It is for this reason, that marriages are under attack. The divorce rate in the U.S. is between 50-60 percent and it's about equal to that in the church. If you've been through a divorce, this is not a condemnation, but this trend has got to change, especially in the Church. After all in the Bible, Jesus is called the Bridegroom and the Church is called the Bride. In other words our human marriages are what's called a "type" representing Jesus' relationship with His Church, with us. If we are to model God's unfailing love to a world who desperately needs Him, our marriages are a great place to start.

I hear people talking about 50-50 marriages. They think this speaks to balance and equality and they are, for the most part, completely and utterly wrong. A 50-50 marriage will end in divorce nearly every time. The reasons are simple. First the Golden Rule comes into play. It says, "Do unto others as you would have them do unto you." Notice it doesn't say "Do unto others AS they do unto you." That's 50-50. It says, "You go so far and I'll meet you half way, but if you fail to meet my expectations, don't expect me to keep up my part of the bargain." Now I know that's the way the world works and it may be good enough to be fair, but is it enough? We get a clearer model for marriage when we go back to the biblical "type." In it, Jesus is the model for the perfect spouse. His love is complete, sacrificial and unconditional. He laid down His life to compensate for our failure. He gave it all, 100 percent, even though we came up way short, and He redeemed us. That's how we need to love one another, especially in marriage, especially among believers and if we loved like that, we would build each other up, and lift each other up, and it would be awesome. Marriages like that would strengthen families, and communities, and eventually the world.

You might be thinking that's great if both parties are believers and committed to following the example of Jesus, but what if one spouse is and the other is not. The Bible calls that "unequally yoked." To get the imagery, you have to think back to ancient agriculture. Back before there were tractors and farm implements, the heavy lifting (okay, more like pulling) was done by beasts of burden, like horses and mules and especially oxen. Two oxen would put their heads through wooden or metal loops that would hang beneath a wooden bar, which would then attach to the wagon or plow. That device was called a "yoke." To pull in a straight line, both oxen had to be fairly equally matched (with some exceptions), and pulling in the same direction. When this occurred, the team of oxen were said to be "equally yoked." In this thing called marriage, the husband and wife are a team and they need to be pulling in the same direction, headed to the same place, otherwise they are said to be "unequally yoked. "

So if that is you, if you're the believing spouse, what do you do? Do you leave? No. 1Peter 3:1-2 (NIV) says, "Wives, in the same way submit yourselves to your own husbands so that, if any of them do not believe the word, they may be won over without words by the behavior of their wives, when they see the purity and reverence of your lives." Let's go around that word "submission" for a moment, we'll get back to it, I promise, and when we do, women, it will be better than you think. For now let's look at the rest of the passage and, by the way, the principle applies to both spouses. Believing spouse, you live your life in a way that honors God, regardless of what your spouse does, because that's what believers do. You look out for your spouse's good and live to be a blessing in hopes that your spouse will come to believe. It's not easy, but it honors God.

Submission and Death

Let's go a little deeper, and to do this we have to talk about submission. There's a passage that I always use in pre-marital counseling and frankly part of the reason I use it, is to see how ready a young man is for marriage. It's found in Ephesians 5:22-24 (NIV). "Wives, submit yourselves to your own husbands as you do to the Lord. For the husband is the head of the wife as Christ is the head of the church, his body, of which he is the Savior. Now as the church submits to Christ, so also wives should submit to their husbands in everything." Now I know that this will have some people growling, but trust me there is more to the story. Stay tuned. Remember again we are dealing with a type. Christ is the Bridegroom, the Church is the Bride. That's our model and so as the Church submits to Jesus, so wives need to submit to their husbands. When I see a young man get all prideful and puffed up about this verse, I start to wonder if he's ready and I will admit, it gives me a little joy to rain on his parade.

You see if he is willing to make his wife a footstool and the lesser partner, he hasn't really considered what marriage is all about.

First of all, I skipped over Ephesians 5:21 (NIV). Submit to one another out of reverence for Christ. This verse talks about mutual submission, and essentially what that means is a husband and wife are supposed to look out for one another. The concept behind marriage is that that the two become one. This should radically change our perspective. All of the sudden, there is someone else in your life and that person and you are completely interdependent. What is good for one spouse is good for the other and so we put the other person first, so wives are supposed to submit to husbands, but husbands are also supposed to submit to their wives, by putting the wife's needs ahead of their own. Yes, I am fully aware that this is a hard thing, because both parties have their flaws and struggles, but this is where the Golden Rule comes in. Remember we can never control what other people do. We can only control what we do. If you want your spouse to give 100 percent, you have to give 100 percent, whether they do or not.

But now we get to the part of the passage that will rain on the parade of an ill-prepared man, Ephesians 5:25-27 (NIV) "Husbands, love your wives, just as Christ loved the church and gave himself up for her to make her holy, cleansing her by the washing with water through the word, and to present her to himself as a radiant church, without stain or wrinkle or any other blemish, but holy and blameless." Husbands you're called to love you wife like Christ loves the Church. Remember, He died for the Church. He laid down His very life for His bride. Wives you are called to submit, but husbands, you're called to die. You're called to love sacrificially. You're called to lay down anything that would be detrimental to your marriage and your wife. You're called to put her needs before your own and look out for her in every aspect of life, and yes, you're called to lay down even your very life for her. Every once in a while, I hear a guy say something to the effect of "Baby, I'd die for you." The odds of you having to do that are pretty slim, so how are you at doing the simpler things that happen every day? Part of our call as husbands, the biggest part, is to love and serve our wives in the day to day, dying to ourselves and living in our marriages submitted to Christ.

The rest of the passage fleshes this out Ephesians 5:28-33 (NIV) "In this same way, husbands ought to love their wives as their own bodies. He who loves his wife loves himself. After all, no one ever hated their own body, but they feed and care for their body, just as Christ does the church— for we are members of his body. "For this reason a man will leave his father and mother and be united to his wife, and the two will become one flesh." This is a profound mystery—but I am talking about Christ and the church. However, each one of you also must love his wife as he loves himself, and the wife must respect her husband." This is how God wants you to treat your wife and how He wants you to love your wife. It's a call to sacrificial love and there is a penalty for getting this wrong.

1 Peter 3:7 (NIV) "Husbands, in the same way be considerate as you live with your wives, and treat them with respect as the weaker partner and as heirs with you of the gracious gift of life, so that nothing will hinder your prayers." Now I know that weaker partner thing is a struggle, I struggle with it too, partly because my wife is a strong woman. In the ideal world, God brings us together with spouses who have strengths where we have weaknesses and weaknesses where we have strengths. I know this works in my own life. As mentioned earlier, I'm an artist, a creative, a real right brainer and so God gave me a wife who is gifted with numbers and accounting. I've helped her to embrace her creative side and she has helped me live more practically. I can prob-

ably bench press more than she can, and she makes sure that we have a roof over our heads. So again the weaker partner part is debatable, but here is what's not. The Bible tells us that if we husbands are not treating our wives properly, our prayers will be hindered. I think the best way to think of this is to think about your daughter. (If you don't have a daughter, imagine you do.) Suppose she meets a guy and he doesn't treat her well. How likely are you to help him? Well, your wife is God's daughter and the same rules apply. How we treat our wives matters.

How about the children? Ephesians 6:1-3 (NIV) Children, obey your parents in the Lord, for this is right. "Honor your father and mother"—which is the first commandment with a promise— "so that it may go well with you and that you may enjoy long life on the earth." There is a command to obey our parents and honor them and this commandment does not have an expiration date. Now please note those words "in the Lord." This means that the obedience has a boundary, and if they are leading you in a way that does not honor God, you are not obligated to follow, but otherwise, we are to obey and to honor. The command does have a promise and we would be wise to follow this admonition. By the way this is a two way street.

Ephesians 6:4 (NIV) "Fathers, do not exasperate your children; instead, bring them up in the training and instruction of the Lord." In other words we are supposed to treat our children well at all times. We're not supposed to exasperate them. We can challenge them to bigger and better things, but we are not supposed to frustrate them or make them feel like they can never be good enough. A lot of our struggles with being enough later in life are formed in the childhood years and those years are of urgent importance. Children need to know that they are loved unconditionally, they need to be nurtured and trained. As Proverbs 22:6 (NIV) says "Start children off on the way they should go, and even when they are old they will not turn from it." They need to know that, to you, they are enough.

Enough

I came to faith and parenthood pretty close to the same time and in the early days of my faith, I had some unusual ideas. One of them was, I wished before Jesus died on the cross, He would have married and had a couple of kids. I really wanted to see how the perfect man did parenthood, largely because this very imperfect man was struggling. Of course I hadn't considered all the ramifications of all of that. Then one day I really began to examine a phrase that's all over the Bible and said so often in the Church that I think we might lose it's significance. We already have an example of the perfect Father. There are children of God running all around our world. I'm one of them. From there, all I had to do was see the unconditional love He has for me. I wish I had seen this sooner, because it would have helped me to realize that in Him I am enough. Fathers, and mothers, we must model that kind of love to our children as we train them to follow God.

Other Relationships

Of course there are a multitude of other relationships in our lives. For example, we're supposed to model God's love to our coworkers. There are several passages that talk about how slaves are supposed to submit to their masters and, because slavery in the ancient world was very different than the hideous thing it was in our American History, there are parallels that can be drawn to our lives as employees and co-workers. Look at Ephesians 6:5-8 (NIV) for example. "Slaves, obey your earthly masters (employers) with respect and fear, and with sincerity of heart, just as you would obey Christ. Obey them not only to win their favor when their eye is on you, but as slaves of Christ, doing the will of God from your heart. Serve wholeheartedly, as if you were serving the Lord, not people, because you know that the Lord will reward each one for whatever good they do, whether they are slave or free." When we do what we do as if we were doing it for God, our good, ethical work becomes ministry to those around us.

And by the way if you're a believing employer or a supervisor, rather than employee, you're not off the hook. Ephesians 6:9 (NIV) says, "And masters, treat your slaves in the same way. Do not threaten them, since you know that he who is both their Master and yours is in heaven, and there is no favoritism with him." We need to make sure that we treat people in a way that honors God.

God calls us to love our friends, our neighbors and even our enemies in a way that honors Him, whether they are believers or not, whether they are kind in return or not, (The Golden Rule, remember?) because how we treat people shows them a lot about what God is like. Consider 1 Peter 2:12 (NIV) for example, "Live such good lives among the pagans that, though they accuse you of doing wrong, they may see your good deeds and glorify God on the day he visits us." The way we live in relationship to others as believers, will give them a glimpse into the character of God. So how we live in the relationships we maintain, is immensely important, because remember God is all about relationships and He desires to be in relationship with all who will call on His name. We live in this world as His ambassadors. Is there ever a time to look at a relationship with someone and say "Enough's enough." It could still happen, but only after every other avenue has been exhausted. We cannot be quick to give up on people, because we represent a God who never gives up on us.

Forgiveness

Now that we've been through these other relationships, let's return to Matthew 18. Peter has been with Jesus through the whole teaching and the proverbial lightbulb of an idea goes off in his head. He knows what this teaching is about. Now at this point, I should tell you, I am a big fan of Peter. He's one of my favorite people from Scripture. I feel like he would be something of a kindred spirit for me. He sometimes charges into situations without thinking. He can be bold and brash. I like all that about him, but did you ever notice when he's around Jesus, he's a different person. When he's around Jesus, all he wants to do is please Jesus. I know it might be impossible for flawed humanity to impress a perfect God, but Peter's still going to try, Peter hears Jesus teaching on conflict resolution and he knows that at the heart of the matter is forgiveness. By the way, this is also key for all of our relationships.

Seventy Times Seven

It almost seems as if he interrupts Jesus. "Master, how many times should I forgive my brother when he sins against me, up to seven times." Now please note, Peter is trying to be impressive here. It is said that the Pharisees demanded that you forgive someone three times. That's it. If someone did something a fourth time, you could write them off. You could wash your hands of them. They were dead to you. As you can imagine this was disastrous. People everywhere had to be keeping tally sheets (at least mental ones) on how many more times people could fail before relationships could be broken. This might be why Paul told us that "love keeps no record of wrongs." Peter in his statement is trying to show Jesus that he is willing to go double what is required, plus one more. Now ordinarily that would be fantastic. If your boss at work required something of you and you doubled it, plus one more, that would be a very good day for all involved, but when Jesus hears Peter's "generous" offer, something different happens. I can almost picture Jesus smiling, shaking his head just a little and saying "No Peter, not seven times but seventy seven times, and some translations say seventy times seven—490 times.

Please don't get caught up in the number. All that would give us is longer tally sheets. What Jesus is really saying is, "I want you to forgive, and then I want you to forgive more, and then I want you to keep on forgiving until you lose count, and then forgive some more." Now I will be the first to admit that is a really tall order. How can Jesus ask so much of us? He can ask for two reasons, first and foremost is because He is God, but the bigger issue is, that is the example He set. That is what He does for us. Forgiving over and over again as we fail over and over again, because our relationship with Him is of paramount importance to Him. Remember He's all about relationships. He doesn't look at us and say. "Enough, I've had it with you." That's part of the reason His grace is so amazing.

The Price of Unforgiveness

Then to punctuate the point, Jesus went into a parable. Remember, He's teaching His disciples here. He spoke of a very wealthy man, who came home from a journey for the purpose of settling accounts with servants who owe him money. The first guy called in owes the master ten thousand talents. A talent was a unit of measure for money. I did some research to see how much the man's debt was. The best way to find this out is to find the value of a single talent and multiply. After extensive research, I can honestly say, I still don't know the value of a biblical talent, because different sources say different things.

One source said a talent was worth a thousand dollars. That's a fair amount of money. Another source said a talent was worth a year's wages, that's even more. Finally another source said a talent was worth 20 years wages. So while the results of my research were inconclusive, to find the value of the man's debt, we just have to do a little math. I know when you hear "Let's do the math," most people's eyes glaze over, but I promise to keep it short.

At the low end, if a talent is worth $1,000, the man's 10,000 talent debt means he owns his master $10,000,000. At the high end, if a talent is worth 20 years wages, the man owes his master 200,000 years wages. I'm pretty sure he's not going to live that long, and that is the point. Remember this is a parable, and not a true story. Jesus was deliberately making the man's debt so ridiculously high that the man could never pay it back. This was the point Jesus wanted to make. The debt of their sin was so high that it could never be repaid. The same is true for us.

Well the man in the parable is in deep, deep trouble. He is quite literally in a hole he could never, ever get out of. Keep in mind, Jesus and His audience live in the first century, not the twenty-first. In the twenty-first, if you are over your head in debt, you have some options. There are debt consolidation loans, payment plans, you can even declare bankruptcy and be absolved of your debt, at least to some degree. In the first century, under the Roman Empire, your choices were substantially less. First century debtors could either be sold into slavery or you could be imprisoned and your family sold into slavery until the debt was paid. This man's debt was so high it could never be repaid. He had only on option. He threw himself on the mercy of his master. He said, "Take pity on me and I'll pay you back everything." No he wouldn't. He couldn't, the debt was just too big. The thing to consider is we do the same thing every time we say "Lord, if you will just get me through this I'll (fill in your favorite un-keepable promise here)."

What we need to see is, when the servant appeals to his master's mercy, he receives mercy. The master absolves him of the debt. Think about that. He walks in the door owing a debt he could never repay, up to 200,000 years wages, but he walks out free. A debt of up to 200,000 years wages wiped away in an instant. The man is free because of tremendous mercy, and one could imagine he would be very, very happy, and he was, for about ten seconds.

When he got outside, the forgiven debtor saw a man who owed him five hundred denarius, My research on this was equally inconclusive, but it is a very payable debt, especially when balanced against 10,000 talents. Now surely when he sees this man who owes such a small debt, he remembers the great mercy he has just received and he shows mercy in return, right? I mean surely he sees the man and thinks, "Well he does owe me, but it's nothing compared to what I was just set free from, so I'll let it go." That's what he does, right? No. Well then surely he approaches the man and sets up a fair and equitable payment plan, right? No! He grabs the man by the throat, throws him up against the wall and says, "Pay me what you owe me, and pay it now!" Unbelievable, right?"

I love how Jesus constructs the story. He has the debtor say practically the same exact words that the forgiven servant just said to his benevolent master. "Take pity on me and I'll pay you back everything." In this case though, the odds of repayment are very likely. Surely now the recently forgiven debtor relents, right? No! He has the man thrown into prison until the debt can be paid. Now to be clear in the first century an action like this would have been within the man's rights, but just because he has a right, doesn't make it right. And this is where the man and me become very much alike. Oh, I'd like to think I'd have the mercy this man clearly did not, but I have a profound inability to do something stupid without other people seeing it, and that's what happens.

The man's fellow servants see this man, a person who has been a very recent recipient of a massive amount of mercy, turn around and be immensely unmerciful. They practically sprint to the master and report what happened. Needless to say, when the master heard what happened he was immensely irritated and called the servant back to him. "So, I just forgave you that massive debt and you couldn't show mercy to someone who owed you a measly could of hundred denarius. Well listen up pal, your debt is reinstated." (That's the Dave Weiss paraphrase.) And he had the man thrown into prison until the whole debt could be repaid. Not only that, but the master states that he is to be tortured until the debt is paid. In essence, that means he would be in prison forever, being tortured forever, since the debt can never be paid, and it is at this point that Jesus said some of the scariest words in all of scripture:

"This is how my heavenly Father will treat each of you unless you forgive your brother or sister from your heart." (Matthew 18:35 NIV)

Let's consider what this means. Jesus just finished telling the story of a man who could not forgive and will now be tortured forever, and again it's just a parable, but Jesus used these parables to teach truth. So does this mean that if we do not forgive, we will lose our salvation. Some will say yes, and those people might be right, but I'm not in that camp and I favor a different point of view. It's one that I think is at least nearly as compelling. Let me start by asking you to do something a little bit painful. I want you to close your eyes and think of someone you can't forgive, or maybe someone you have a hard time forgiving.

Do you have them in your mind?

Okay, now let me ask you a follow up question. What happens every time you see that person? What happens every time you think about that person? Don't you get to remember and in a sense live through the thing they did to you, in your heart and mind, over and over again. They may have moved on, or maybe even passed on, but you get to experience it, at least emotionally, over and over again. How much different is that than being tortured? The thing is God has given us a way out of that. It's called forgiveness. See the dirty little secret about forgiveness is it is, at least in part, and probably mainly, for you. Forgiveness frees you from having to experience the pain over and over again.

What Forgiveness Is Not

Now I know this is hard. I've been through some stuff too, and no, I don't want to compare "war stories." That's counter productive. We all have our own scars, and they wounded us in the ways that they did and brought us the pain that they did. Each experience is unique to each individual and nothing I've written here is meant to minimize your pain. I'm just trying to show you the way to freedom. We also need to say a word or two about what forgiveness is not. Forgiveness doesn't mean you can't go to the authorities if someone is doing you harm. It also doesn't mean you stay in a situation where you are in danger. It doesn't mean you're a doormat or that you should remain a victim. Forgiveness is none of those things. If you are experiencing abuse, it's time to say "Enough" and sometimes you have to forgive from a distance, but you do have to forgive.

Forgiveness is taking difficult situations and difficult people and giving them to God. It's saying, "Lord, I can't deal with this anymore, and I give it to you. If you want to forgive this person and lead them to repentance, great. If you want to make them pay, so much the better. (That last part was tongue in cheek, but it's the real way we feel sometimes, isn't it?) They are yours now to do with as you want. I choose to forgive. Help me to forgive. I want to be free." When we give the people and the situations over to God and leave them with Him, and don't keep going back for them, we can be free. That is the true power of forgiveness.

Who Do You Need to Forgive?

And now I need to ask you a follow up question. Who do you need to forgive? Who is that person you saw when you closed your eyes? It's time to stop carrying that around. It's time to say "Enough!" to reliving the trauma, or the drama they created in your life. It's time to give them over to God, so you can be free. Trust God to restore what He desires to restore and be free.

Forgiving God

Some of you need to forgive God. I can almost hear your blasphemy detectors going off from here. You're thinking, "How can he say that? God is perfect. God never sins. God never does anything wrong." By the way, I agree with every one of those things, so let me ask a follow up question. "Then why are you mad at him? Because many people are. I know I was.

When I was forty years old, I was pastoring a church plant and I was working like crazy. The church couldn't sustain my income so I was what they call "bivocational." As a little aside, my spell check always highlights that word. Maybe for good reason. Bivocational should be temporary. The workman is worthy of his hire, but I digress. Bivocational was my reality. I worked all day at a day job, and spent most of my remaining time working on the church. I would get up early and go to bed late and it took it's toll. One day, after having been sick for a few days, I began having pains in my chest. I didn't think much of it. It wasn't excruciating, but it was Saturday, and I was supposed to go on a lengthy trip the following Monday, so I decided to go to the E.R. to get checked out. I figured I would get some meds, go home and take them and be ready for my trip. My symptoms were so mild, I was shocked when they said, "Mr. Weiss, do you realize you're having a heart attack?" "I do now!" I thought.

As they rushed around, figuring out how to keep me from going into a much worse situation, I got more and more scared. Then conflicting voices came into the back of my mind. I heard the voice of a woman from years before who questioned the salvation of a friend because in the midst of an illness, she feared death. That voice put questions in my head "Is there something wrong with my faith?" "Am I really saved?" I heard all kinds of other stuff, guilt and condemnation. I thought of my sons. My oldest was just about to be married. Would I live to see the wedding? My youngest was ten, who would care for him, and what would happen if I died?" Fear and anxiety were manifesting in big ways and then a new emotion came—anger. I would have understood all of this that I was going through back in the day, when I was mistreating my body with alcohol, but now I was working hard for the Lord, and how could He let this happen to me?

Theologians call it the retribution principle and it's really easy to fall into. The basic idea is good people deserve good and bad people deserve bad, and in my mind at that moment, God was unjust. I didn't deserve this. Right now theologians want to scream at me, so let me just be clear. My rational mind knows that the retribution principle doesn't always work in the Kingdom of God. I also know that Jesus came so that we would not get what we ultimately deserve, and further, I know that God is good regardless of what happens to me. My rational mind knows all of that stuff, but at that moment I was not rational. I was sad, scared and mad and it took a long time to get over all of that. I felt like God had let me down. Pair that with a medication, that was causing my surface chest muscles to tighten at the slightest provocation and you get the idea. It was a really bad time for me. I was mad at God and I was trying to pastor a church while I sorted it out. That was not an easy thing to do.

And then one day, it broke. I realized I couldn't go on like that anymore, something had to give so I did something that seemed ridiculous even to me in that state of mind. I forgave God. Now to be clear, I knew He didn't need my forgiveness. I knew in my heart all of this was actually my problem. but I went to God in prayer and said something to the effect of, "I don't know why you left this happen, but there's a wall between us and I'm pretty sure I put it there. God, I still love you. I still trust you, even if it doesn't look like it and I know you don't need it, but I don't know what else to do, so I forgive you." That was when the healing really began. In my spirit, I began to hear the still small voice of God. He was saying things like "David, did I ask you to work that hard? No, I didn't. That was you. Did I tell you you couldn't rest? No, I didn't. That was you. Who asked you to work like it all depends on you? It wasn't me. It doesn't all depend on you. It depends on me and you depend on me." He took me through my questions. He reminded me that as much as I love my sons, He loves them more and that He can be depended on to take care of them better than I can and when it was done there was one last thing to do. I needed to ask God to forgive me, which was kind of the point all along.

I know today that mild heart attack saved my life and my ministry. I take better care of myself today (well at least most of the time). I've learned to rest (most of the time) and I am more convinced than ever of who this all depends on and who I depend on and that He can always be depended upon. Do you need to forgive God today? He hasn't let you down. Fear and pain and anxiety might be telling you something different, but this much I can tell you from experience. He has never left your side and He is waiting for you to come around. He has never stopped loving you and He never will. If you're mad at God, well He can handle that, but you can't. Go to Him and talk it out. Take Him everything. He can take it and then just listen and don't stop listening until you hear Him. He will never leave nor forsake you. He wants to restore the relationship. He wants you back.

The Person You May Need to Forgive the Most

Finally there is one other person, you may need to forgive. This person has made choices that are likely to drive you crazy, and for many people, those choices have messed them up more than any other. In many people's lives, this person needs more forgiveness than anyone. It should come as no surprise that the person in question is you. Most people need to forgive themselves and this is a crucial factor in what it means to be enough. If you can't forgive yourself, it is likely to hold you back in virtually every area of your life.

If this is you, I have to start off with a simple question. Have you asked Jesus Christ to be your Lord and Savior? Have you trusted that what He did on the cross, He did for you? If you haven't, that's the first step. If you have and you still can't forgive yourself. There is only one question left. Why? I mean He laid down His life so you could be forgiven and if you have trusted in Him then you are forgiven. In other words, He has already forgiven you. So if you feel unforgiven, you have to realize that the problem is you. God has said that he puts our sin as far as the east is from the west. Do you believe God means what He says? Then you are forgiven by the One who matters most. The only thing left to do is for you to forgive you and if you forgive you, and God forgives you, you are free, but not just free, permanently free. In Christ, you're forgiven, you've received grace, and you're enough.

Enough

10
Am I Loved Enough?
Exploring God's Love

Did you ever come to a place where you wonder if God still loves you? Maybe it's the result of some circumstances that are going against you or maybe it's the result of your own actions and the condemnation you feel as a result. What you need to know is that God's love for you is unconditional. Now you can reject Him and reject His love, but if you have come to Jesus, believe in what He did for you on the cross, and if you accept that He did that for you, you will be saved and live forever with Him in paradise. We'll get to that more in a minute, but first we need to look at a verse.

1 John 4:18 (NIV) says, "There is no fear in love. But perfect love drives out fear, because fear has to do with punishment. The one who fears is not made perfect in love." I have wrestled with the meaning of this passage for a long time. There was a time in my life where I worried that I wasn't loved because I was afraid at times. When you're already afraid, thoughts like this will paralyze you, but here's the thing, fear and wisdom are pretty closely linked and wisdom is lauded all over the Scriptures. For example, if you're at the zoo and you see a way to jump into the lion enclosure, but you're afraid to do that, congratulations! You're living wisdom. If you find yourself in a perfectly good airplane and you decide it might not be prudent to jump out, congratulations! You're living in wisdom.

But there's more to fear. I can't speak for you, but while agree that perfect love drives out fear, some of my greatest fears arise from the people I love the most. From knowing my sons are out on snowy and icy roads to the world that we are handing off to my grandson, there are a lot of things that can peg my fear meter. Does 1 John 4:18 mean I don't love because I have fears? More importantly, do my fears mean God doesn't love me? I don't think so. And then one day, I had a revelation, perfect love drives out fear, but I'm not capable of perfect love. I mean, try as I might, and I do try, I occasionally hurt the ones I love and sometimes even if I don't hurt them, I realize I don't always serve them the way a loving person would. These are people I would lay down my life for, and yet sometimes even the simplest of services feel like too much. My love even on my best days is far from perfect.

So what is this "perfect love" the passage speaks of? The only place anything truly perfect can come from is the only truly perfect person. The only perfect love is God's love and God's love is truly and completely perfect. If we truly understood this, it would radically change our lives. Some people live in fear because they think that if they make a mistake (or too many mistakes), that God will stop loving them. The reason for this is pretty simple, we assign human qualities to God, but God is better than us. God is perfect and so is His love. Nothing you do can make Him love you any less than the perfect love that He feels for each of us. Nothing! So don't be afraid. You are loved.

The other side of this is for the people pleasers in our world. They assign the quality of being unappeasable to God. You know, we have people in our lives whose love is conditioned on what we do, If we do more, they love us more, we do less and they love us less. That's not how God works. While nothing we can do can make Him love us any less, nothing we can do can make Him love us any more. This is the true meaning of unconditional love. His love is perfect. It cannot be greater or less because either of those things would imply imperfection. He is perfect. God's word tells us, God and Jesus Christ are the same yesterday, today and forever. His love will never change. His love for you will never change, ever. It's perfect. Perfect means perfect and perfect love is enough—better yet, more than enough.

When the passage says perfect love drives out fear, and it is beyond my capacity to love perfectly, then the perfect love that drives out fear is not my flawed love, it's God's perfect love. It speaks of fear having to do with punishment. Again, this deals with assigning human flaws to a flawless God. Deep down our fears, at least in regard to God, are fears that He will give up on us and cast us out. We may have been treated by people that way, or at least have been made to feel that way by other people, but God is different. God never gives up on us. He never falls out of love with us, or loses feelings for us or any of those other things that humans have perpetrated on us. God's love is perfect. It is never taken from us. We only lose it if we reject it by rejecting the ultimate act of love.

Love Requires a Choice

Our troubles started at the beginning. They started in the Garden, with our first parents Adam and Eve. They were created to be in a close personal relationship with God. They (and we) were created to love God and to be loved perfectly by God. The thing with love though is it requires a choice. When I officiate a wedding, there comes a point in every service where I say to a young woman, "forsaking all others do you take this man to be your lawfully wedded husband?" It sounds so nice and formal, but did you ever think about what it actually means? What I'm really saying to her is, "You realize there are about 3.5 billion men in the world? Are you really sure you want this one? Really? You're sure?" Okay that was a little facetious, but ultimately that is the choice. Do you choose to love this person? If there are no choices, is it really love? Well God gave our first parents a choice. The choice was not another person, not another god (there is no other god). It was a tree.

The choice was simple. They were taken through the garden and shown all the beautiful trees with all their beautiful fruit and God told them they could eat from any of them..

well any, but not the one in the middle. That tree was the tree of the knowledge of good and evil. They were instructed to stay away from that one or they would die. The meaning and the choice were simple. God was saying, "If you love me, stay away from that tree. Love me enough to stay away." It didn't last long. Temptation came to call and with it, a lie. It was a three-fold attack from the enemy of our souls. It's the same attack he has used ever since. He started off with a question. "Did God really say you cannot eat from any tree in the garden?" Step one: Get people to question whether or not God means what He says. Eve answered correctly. "No we can eat from any tree but that one. If we eat from that one, we'll die" It's here that we get to step two: Contradict God. "You will surely not die. God is lying to you," which leads almost directly to step three: God is not good. "God knows that when you eat of it, you'll be like Him. God doesn't want that, because God is not good. God is withholding His best from you." Three simple questions and our first parents fell for it. It's the same three-step process Satan has used ever since and he uses it because it continually works almost every time.

Ultimately the question is a question of God's love. Does God love us, is He good and can we trust Him? Fortunately, the answer to all three of those questions is "Yes." God is good, He does love you and you can trust Him completely.

The funny thing is there was a small portion of truth in what the enemy said. There was something that God was withholding from them. Remember, what the tree was called? The tree of the knowledge of good and evil. The tree stood right in the middle of the Garden of Eden. That word "Eden" means "delight. "Adam and Eve lived in the very presence of God, basking in His love, each and every day, in the Garden of "Delight." Translation—they know good. They were surrounded in goodness and perfect love. What God was actually depriving them of was the knowledge of evil. Oh, the horror. Had they trusted His love, goodness and truth, they (and we) could have lived in a world without the knowledge of evil.

That of course, did not happen. Eve, and Adam who was with her, ate from the tree and were cast out of the Garden. "Wait," you might be thinking. "I thought you said God would never stop loving us." I did and I stand by it. "Then why did God cast them out of the garden?" Because they did what God told them not to do. God is ultimately loving AND ultimately just. Just because God loves us, does not mean actions and choices, do not have consequences. This is a fundamental misunderstanding many people have. They get the idea that if something bad happens, God has walked out on them. This is not the case. Bad times are not a reflection of a lack of love on God's part. Sin is a reflection of a lack of love on ours. God still loves perfectly.

In the garden was the Tree of Life. Eat from that tree and you will live forever, but God said if they ate from the Tree of the Knowledge of Good and Evil, that they would die. God's unchanging justice and love, meant that the consequences He stated must be carried out. When they lost the garden, they lost physical immortality. Consequences came, but love remains.

Sin separates us from God because God is perfect and we are not. It happened in the garden and we have been separated ever since but from before time began, God already had a plan to deal with our sin and that separation. He loves us so much, that, at just the right time, He sent His one and only Son, to die for our sins and restore the relationship. It was the ultimate act of love from the one whose love is more than enough.

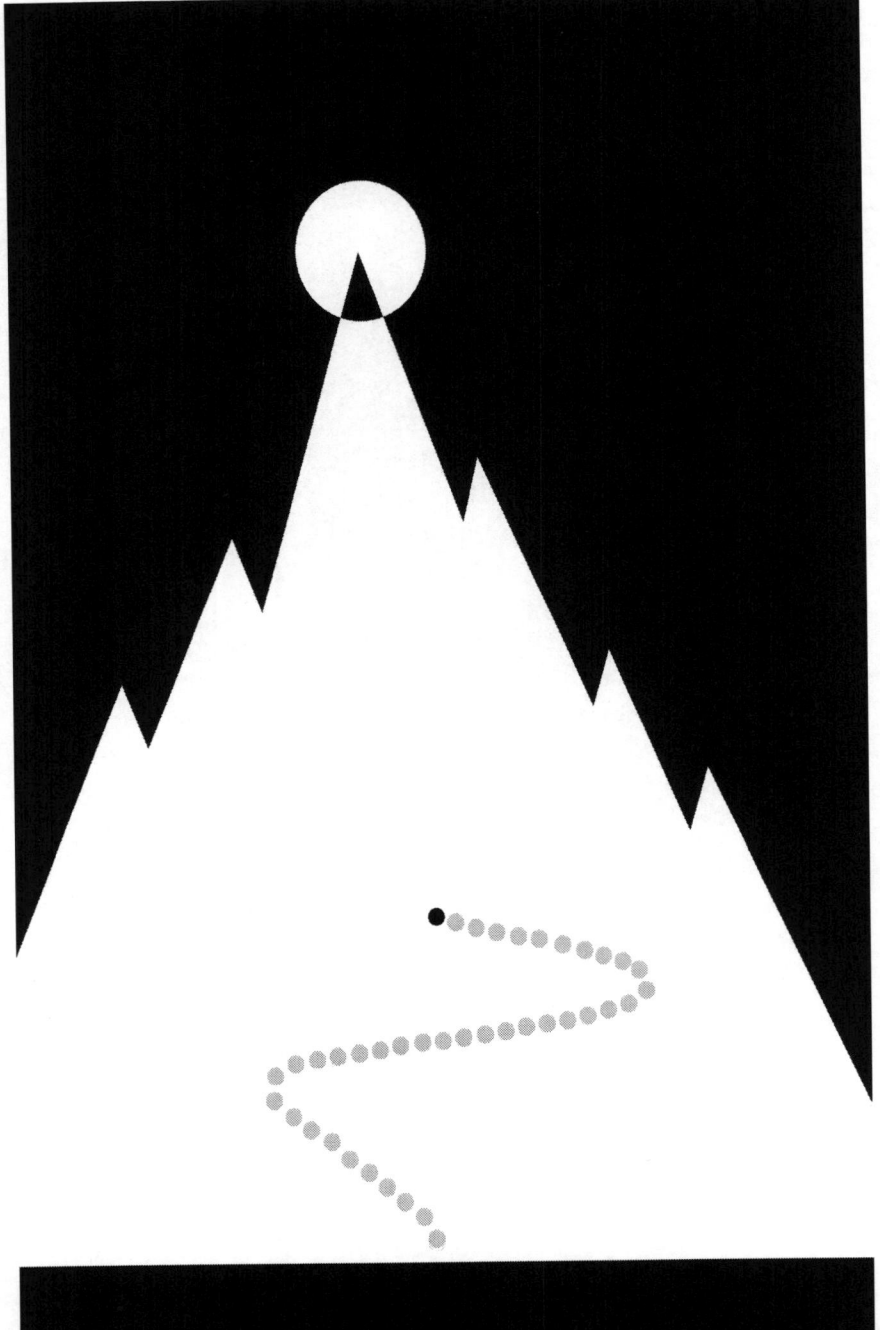

11
Great enough?
Exploring Our Position in God's Kingdom

One of the things many people strive for in this world is greatness. We want to be great at what we do, and there is nothing wrong with that, well except for one thing. What does the word "great" mean and who defines greatness? The answers to those questions is crucial, because without that knowledge, the quest for greatness can leave us, once again feeling like we'll never be enough.

You see greatness is subjective. To illustrate this, let's consider one of the most subjective things there is, art. What constitutes great art? I use this example often when I do art presentations. People will come up to me after a presentation and say "I can't do art." They think that's true, but it's not really what they mean. What they really mean is they can't reach a level in art where they can look at their work and think, "That's great!" Pablo Picasso once said, "All children are artists, the problem is to remain one as one grows up." These people who think they can't make art have not lost the physical ability to do art, they've lost the mental or emotional ability to love what they make. They'll often say things like "I can't draw a straight line," or "I can't draw a stick figure." My usual flippant, but totally sincere response is, "Then don't draw straight lines and stick figures." I then tell them to go to an art museum. At the average art museum, you will see work that you couldn't do if you lived to be a million. By contrast, you will see other work that looks like anyone could have done it, or makes you question why anyone would do it. I know that makes me sound like an artistic cretin, but, I'm sorry, it's true and the person will nearly always agree. Then I tell them two things, first of all their level of ability will be found somewhere between the extremes, and secondly, all the works in that museum are there because someone, somewhere, considered them to be great.

Now to be clear, I'm not trying to make you into an artist, nor am I saying that anyone and everyone can be a professional artist. I'm saying greatness in art and in all aspects of life is subjective. One man's trash is another man's treasure and part of achieving greatness in what we do is finding our best areas of gifting. Everyone, I repeat, everyone is gifted. Once we find that area of gifting, our responsibility moves to developing our gifts to the best of our ability. From there it's a matter of doing our best work and finding the people who are blessed by it. This is crucial. You will never please everyone all the time. The only way to even come close, is to embrace mediocrity and do things that are so "vanilla" that no one will be bothered or take offense. The thing is mediocre, by it's very definition, is not great. Instead we all need to put our work and our best selves out for all the world to see, while looking for the ones who resonate with it. It is likely you'll be great in someone's eyes, but probably not in everyone's eyes.

In some ways this is antithetical to the way most people live. See if this seems familiar. You do something in public. You put yourself out there in front of, say 100 people and poll them afterwards to see what they thought. 99 of those people say it was fantastic and one person said it was awful. Which of those responses draws your attention? Which one sticks with you? For most of my life, I wanted to create to silence the critics. In the above scenario, I would have been so focused on the one critic, that I would have missed all the people who loved what I did. As a result of that tendency, I always found myself creating to show that one person that my work has value. That's called being a "people pleaser" and it was the fast track to feeling like I was never enough. When it comes to what we do, we need to bring our best to the ones who love our work and forget the rest.

Let's consider an example. I don't like rap music. There's nothing wrong with it. I appreciate that it's a complex art form and it takes a lot of skill. I'm just not a fan. Should (fill in your favorite rapper here) go out of his or her way to create an album of music I'd like? No, He or she has a million fans in his or her genre that love his or her work (work that is true to he or she is as an artist) as it is. To flip genres to please me would be a fool's errand for two reasons. First of all, jumping to a genre I like, will most likely require moving way outside his or her wheelhouse. Chances are awfully good that he or she will not succeed in creating something that is on par with people in that genre who are working in their wheelhouse, so I probably still won't like it. Let's assume though, that they do the crossover successfully and they create something that I do like, maybe even love. I would be happy, but the millions of people who love their music, right now, as it is, are probably going to hate it. To make one person happy they would have to make their legion of fans unhappy. It's simply not worth it to create for the critics and greatness will not be found there. If you want to be great at what you do, the best path is to do what you do best, to the best of your ability and work to please the people who love it.

The Scourge of Excellence

There is a word that makes me cringe, especially in the Church, and that word is "excellence." Every time I go to a conference and hear someone talk about the way they strive for excellence, I have a strong desire to leave the room, partly because it irritates me and mostly because I want to start making rather loud commentary. I can almost hear what you're thinking from here. "I think you're wrong. We need excellence in the church. We're supposed to do everything to the glory of God, right? God is not glorified in mediocre." Are you sure?

Next you'll want to point me to the "special music" many churches do, that involves "Aunt Erma." Aunt Erma is a faithful servant, but she can't carry a tune in a bucket. It's so bad that it grates on the nerves of everyone, except Aunt Erma. "What if a visitor has to sit through that? They'll never be back. That's why we need excellence."

Consumer Mentality

Here's the problem, excellence is like greatness and enough. Its a sliding scale and a slippery slope. How do people become excellent? They learn and grow. How can they learn and grow if every opportunity for learning and growth is choked out in the pursuit of excellence? We wonder why the Church has a consumer mentality. I can tell you why. No one has the opportunity to contribute except the talented few that can meet the sliding scale of excellence. The rest come to the church to sit in their seats and watch the show, Why shouldn't they be consumers when all we will allow them to do is consume? The other side of this is how much do we excuse in the lives of the "excellent" simply because of their talent? For example, if "Joe" is a virtuoso guitarist but he's living a sinful mess of a life, how long are you going to put him up in front of the congregation? His talent is excellent, but where will his example lead? Excellence can be a very bad thing.

But what if we considered excellence differently? What if instead of only using the people who've arrived, we gave the inexperienced the opportunity to learn and grow? What if we considered excellence to be the best you can do today? What if we let people start where they are, and help them to demonstrate faithfulness in the way they work toward growth? What if character counted more than talent? By the way, character does count more than talent, especially in the Church. If we looked at excellence in this way, we wouldn't constantly ne looking for people to serve. There would be a point of entry for the talented beginner and the person who just wants to try. Character flaws could be worked out and everyone could start to feel "great" about where they are in the journey.

Yes, I hear you again. You're saying, "But you haven't addressed Aunt Erma?" One of the things to consider is Aunt Erma is a faithful servant. She sings because she has always sung. She may not be in her talent zone, and no, she will never be a great singer, but she is faithful and faithful people can usually be lovingly steered into other avenues. Someone needs to love on her, recognize her faithfulness and help her to grow to find her better place of service. She may not be in her talent zone, but there are areas where she is great. Honor those and help her move toward her place of most effective service. Whatever you do, don't use her as a bad example because, for the most part, she's a good example, maybe even a great one. There's a lot more to being great than talent.

In some cases we also want to be great in the eyes of other people. This can be a little more problematic, especially in the Church. First of all, wanting to great in the eyes of people is hard. People tend to be a little fickle and getting our identity from people can create all kinds of chaos in our lives. We've all met people pleasers. They will do just about anything to make others happy, and you may think that's great and it can be great, if it sticks with a loving attitude and a servant's heart, but we all know people who have taken this to extremes. People pleasers have a hard road ahead of them, because they get their identity from the opinions of others, and that only works as long as they can keep everybody happy. Of course we all know that's easier said than done. Fall out of someone's favor and a people pleaser's world can feel like it's crashing down all around them.

Then there are the other people who want to be great in the eyes of other people, so they do all kinds of things to get attention, or at worst, bully people into submission. These people can become extremely demanding and the pressure of being around them can be devastating. They create relational chaos everywhere they go in their quest for attention, and or dominance. We've all seen these people clash with

121

those in authority or push people down if they're in authority. We saw this in the Scribes and Pharisees in the first century. They were so convinced of their own greatness, that they completely missed the Greatest of all when He stood in their midst. Worse they opposed Him and plotted to kill Him. Think about this. These were the people in authority, religious authority. Their Scriptures, the ones they thought they knew like the backs of their hands, and would have pridefully told you so, foretold His arrival in a multitude of ways. Jesus' arrival should have been the greatest news ever for them, but by now they had important positions, positions of power, and in order for them to hold onto that power, the Messiah became inconvenient and had to go. They were great in their own eyes, and in the eyes of the people. Someone greater coming was not going to work in their plan. They didn't even take the time to investigate His claims. They should have fallen down before Him in worship, but their pride and lust for greatness, made them plot to put Him to death instead. The quest for greatness can get ugly, but Jesus showed a better way.

How Do We Become Great in the Kingdom of God

The disciples of Jesus had similar struggles. They were all sort of looking at each other, trying to figure out which of them were the greatest. They still expected that Jesus would have an earthy kingdom and they were trying to, in a manner of speaking, figure out who would get the corner offices in the palace. It got to the point where the mother of James and John went to Jesus and asked that her sons would get to sit at His right and left hand. In other words, she wanted them to be number two and three in the Kingdom behind Jesus. She wanted her sons to have some sort of earthly power and authority. Now it's unclear whether or not James and John put her up to it, or if we are seeing the first recorded example of a "helicopter mom," but it definitely appears from Jesus' response, that James and John were with her when she brought it up.

"You don't know what you are asking," Jesus said to *them*. (Matthew 20:22A NIV emphasis added.) Jesus is not only speaking to an overreaching mom, but the sons are right there in the midst. It should come as no surprise, but Jesus was right. They had no comprehension of what they were asking for. They simply wanted to be great in the Kingdom. In turn, Jesus asked them if they can drink the cup He is going to drink. They probably thought this would be some mythical gilded chalice around a table in a palace, rather than the cup of suffering Jesus was about to drink on a cross. Jesus further takes them to task and prophetically reveals to them the cup of suffering will be for them as well , but that the Father is the one dealing our right and left hand seats.

Not only did James and John go with their mother as this request was made, but it was made within earshot of the other disciples, who are now extremely angry. Don't feel too bad for them though, they're angry because they all think they are entitled to those seats. There are several times in Scripture, all the way down to the evening of the last supper when the disciples are jockeying for position. Look at Jesus' response:

Jesus called them together and said, "You know that the rulers of the Gentiles lord it over them, and their high officials exercise authority over them. Not so with you. Instead, whoever wants to become great among you must be your servant, and whoever wants to be first must be your slave— just as the Son of Man did not come to be served, but to serve, and to give his life as a ransom for many." (Matthew 20:25-28 NIV)

I'm sure that's not what they had in mind, but this is how it works in the Kingdom of God. Power and position in the Kingdom of God have nothing to do with worldly power and position. We want to climb the ladder in life so that we can stop serving and start being served. We want to get to the place where we're too good for menial things. Greatness demands to be served in the kingdom of the world but in the Kingdom of God, to be great is to humbly serve. If you want to be great in God's Kingdom you have to roll up your sleeves and be a servant of all. Our great example, Lord and Savior, Jesus set that bar for us. He came to serve and then to give His life.

The Full Extent

Consider the last supper. In John 13 we see Jesus with the disciples on that Thursday night getting ready to eat the Passover. John 13:1 (NIV) says "Jesus knew that the hour had come for him to leave this world and go to the Father. Having loved his own who were in the world, he loved them to the end." This verse is from the most recent version of the New International Version of the Bible. The passage I memorized, from the 1984 version, is preferable to me and for this exercise I would like to share it. It's pretty much the same up to the point where it says, "Having loved His own who were in the world," but then it says, "He showed them the full extent of His love." Try to wrap your head around that, Jesus is about to show the full extent of His love. How would that work?

Well, follow the logic for a second. Jesus is the second person of the Trinity, so that makes Him part of the Godhead and, in fact, God. Now the Scriptures say in 1 John 4:8 (NIV) that "God is love." So if Jesus is God personified and God is love, then Jesus is love personified. How does love personified show "the full extent of His love?" Surely, He'll do some massive miracle. Maybe, he'll paint it on the sky or do some kind of mass healing miracle or some big showy expansive, explosive thing, right? I mean this is love personified showing us love to the fullest. This has got to be remarkable.

Well, in a sense it is. Remarkable means literally worth remarking (or talking) about and in that sense, what Jesus did is remarkable. All the preparations had been made for the Passover, except one. In the first century, the main mode of transportation for people was walking. Their primary footwear were sandals. These streets that they walked were probably a combination of stone and dirt. They shared these streets with beasts of burden who left behind all the things that cows and horses and donkeys still leave behind and probably in large quantities. Sanitation in the cities, while advanced for the time, was nowhere near what it is today. The end result of this is, by the end of the day, a person's feet would be mired in filth. For this reason when you entered someone's home, the first thing you would do was wash your feet. If the homeowner had any means, there would be a servant there to wash your feet, and given the disgustingness of the job, it usually fell to the low man on the totem pole. Well when they were doing all the preparations for the Passover feast, none of the disciples made preparations for the washing of feet and this was how Jesus showed the full extend of His love. Not by doing some big showy miracle, but with a humble act of service.

Jesus took off his outer garment and wrapped a towel around His waist and began going down the line of disciples washing their feet. He got all the way down the line to Peter, and it's at this point that Peter has a revelation. This is very, very wrong. There were at least 13 people in that room, and out of all those people, the greatest of all was doing the work usually reserved for the lowest ranking servant in a household. This was not right. Why didn't Peter think to wash feet, or, for that matter, any of the others? The answer, I think, is simple. They were too busy jockeying for position. They all wanted to be the most important. They all thought themselves too good to be the foot washer, but now as the washing begins, Peter sees something is out of whack and he tries to make a change. "He came to Simon Peter, who said to him, "Lord, are you going to wash my feet?" (John 13:6 NIV) It looks like Peter is a little bewildered and the reasons for his bewilderment are hopefully obvious. "Jesus replied, "You do not realize now what I am doing, but later you will understand." (John 13:7A NIV) Ah, there's a lesson here. Jesus is using this action, as an object lesson, at least to some degree, but Peter still has a problem.

"No," said Peter, "you shall never wash my feet." (John 13:7B NIV) Now I have to tell you, Peter's response is right for so many reasons. The greater is serving the lesser. In our world, that's not usually how this works. By now Peter believes Jesus to be the Messiah (though he is still unclear what that really means). He at least knows Jesus is a King and Kings don't wash their servant's feet, or anyone else's for that matter. There is, however one reason why Peter's response is wrong, and it's huge. Peter rightly believes that Jesus is Lord, and you don't say "no" to a Lord. The only proper response to a Lord, especially THE Lord is "Yes Lord!"

I love this next part. "Jesus answered, "Unless I wash you, you have no part with me." (John 13:8 NIV) Jesus knows this lesson is going to be essential to these disciples. They are going to be the ones who take His Gospel to the ends of the earth. These are going to be the first leaders of the Church of Jesus Christ. Their only example of religious leadership, beside Jesus, are the high and mighty Pharisees and Sadducees and their leadership example has been disastrous. When he hears what Jesus has to say, Peter responds properly: "Then, Lord," Simon Peter replied, "not just my feet but my hands and my head as well!" (John 13:9 NIV) Actually Peter goes overboard, but at least now, he's on board.

Next there is a touching moment that we might miss, but it shows a further example of the full extent of Jesus' love. It's found in verse 12A (NIV). "When he had finished washing their feet, he put on his clothes and returned to his place. "Do you understand what I have done for you?" he asked them." Did you catch it? It's the sixth word—the word "their. " Earlier in the chapter, we read that Judas Iscariot had already made the plot to betray Jesus to death and Jesus knew it, and still He washed their feet, all of them, even Judas, even His betrayer. He showed the full extent of His love to them all, even Judas, in what was surely a final act of mercy. That is love to the extreme.

The question is not just a question for them, but for us. "Do you understand what I have done for you?" he asked them. "You call me 'Teacher' and 'Lord,' and rightly so, for that is what I am. Now that I, your Lord and Teacher, have washed your feet, you also should wash one another's feet. I have set you an example that you should do as I have done for you. Very truly I tell you, no servant is greater than his master, nor is a messenger greater than the one who sent him. Now that you know these things, you will be blessed if you do them. (John 13:12B-17 NIV)

Do you understand? He was their leader, their teacher and frankly their better, in every way, (He is God, remember) and still He knelt to serve them in a most humble and humiliating way. He was doing a complete role reversal. The greatest doing the work of the least. The master serving the servant and He commands them to do the same. He is calling them, and us, to servant leadership. The leader needs to be the servant and if we will follow His lead, and lead by serving, we will be blessed. You want to be great? Serve.

Like a Little Child

Being a servant is not what we think of when we pursue greatness is it? Then maybe we should ask ourselves what kind of greatness we're pursuing? Look at Matthew 18:1 (NIV) "At that time the disciples came to Jesus and asked, "Who, then, is the greatest in the kingdom of heaven?" It's another instance of them jockeying for position. It's almost as if they were asking, "Jesus, what are our current rankings and how can we move up the ladder?" By now we should probably be seeing that that's the wrong question, but still Jesus gives us the answer.

Matthew 18:2-5 (NIV) "He called a little child to him, and placed the child among them. And he said: "Truly I tell you, unless you change and become like little children, you will never enter the kingdom of heaven. Therefore, whoever takes the lowly position of this child is the greatest in the kingdom of heaven. And whoever welcomes one such child in my name welcomes me." How do we change and become like little children? Well for starters, little children have an easier time believing without question and we should do the same, trusting God, rather than having to have everything figured out. Little children have an easier time taking things on faith. Further, when He speaks of taking the lowly position of a little child, He probably means we stop jockeying for position and we get humble. It also means we humble ourselves to welcome the little child and all those who might be seen by the world as beneath us. Finally consider how much a child can reward you for helping them. For the most part, they have no means of compensating us. What we do for them is done out of the kindness of our hearts. When we start to serve with no thought of "What's in it for me?" we are getting closer to greatness.

Jesus was a servant leader and He calls us to do the same. He calls us to humble service and demonstrates that true greatness is found in service and humility. In some ways when compared to the way our world works, it appears that God's Kingdom is upside down, but if it looks that way, we're truly looking at it backwards. God's Kingdom is the right way and greatness is found in us turning the world upside down.

Sheep, Goats and the Least of These

There's one last thing to consider. Jesus ends His Olivet Discourse with a story of sheep and goats. He places the sheep on the right and the goats on the left. Now to be clear these are not really livestock, they're people, but they're separated as a shepherd would separate the sheep from the goats. Sheep and goats were often pastured together in the ancient world but they had different needs, especially at night, and so they had to be separated at times. Similarly, the "sheep people" and the "goat people" had different attributes.

Jesus (the King) looks to the people on the right and says, "Come, you who are blessed by my Father; take your inheritance, the kingdom prepared for you since the creation of the world. For I was hungry and you gave me something to eat, I was thirsty and you gave me something to drink, I was a stranger and you invited me in, I needed clothes and you clothed me, I was sick and you looked after me, I was in prison and you came to visit me." (Matthew 25:34B-36 NIV)

Look at all the wonderful things he attributes to these people. They have served humbly and He is pleased with them and calls them blessed. They seem to be dumbfounded by this praise as if they had no idea that had done any of this for Him. "'Lord, when did we see you hungry and feed you, or thirsty and give you something to drink? When did we see you a stranger and invite you in, or needing clothes and clothe you? When did we see you sick or in prison and go to visit you?' (Matthew 25:37-39 NIV) They never saw him even once in these states. He is a king, regal and majestic, surely he has never found himself in most of these predicaments and they didn't remember attending to Him in the few He might have experienced. His response is a lesson for us all.

"Truly I tell you, whatever you did for one of the least of these brothers and sisters of mine, you did for me." (Matthew 25:40B NIV) What you did for the least of these, for those in humble circumstances, especially your brothers and sisters in Christ, was done for Him and so it is with us. He came into this world to serve and not to be served and He expects the same from His followers. Meet the needs of the people around us, as He gives opportunity.

The goats, were the opposite, they did not do what the sheep did and this was to their detriment, their eternal detriment, but we're not going to go further with that. Instead we're going to stick with our theme of being great enough.

In the Kingdom of God to be great is to be a servant. To be great is to be humble. To be great is to serve. In the rest of the world great is fleeting, it's subjective and it's limited, after all there can only be one greatest in any given field at any one time and the competition for the greatest is fierce. In God's Kingdom, greatness is open to anyone who will take the time to care, humble themselves and serve. The field is wide open and there is more need every single day. To be great in God's Kingdom is to look for the opportunity to make even a small difference, humbly. So if you are giving your time to humble service, as God fgives opportunity, you are great enough.

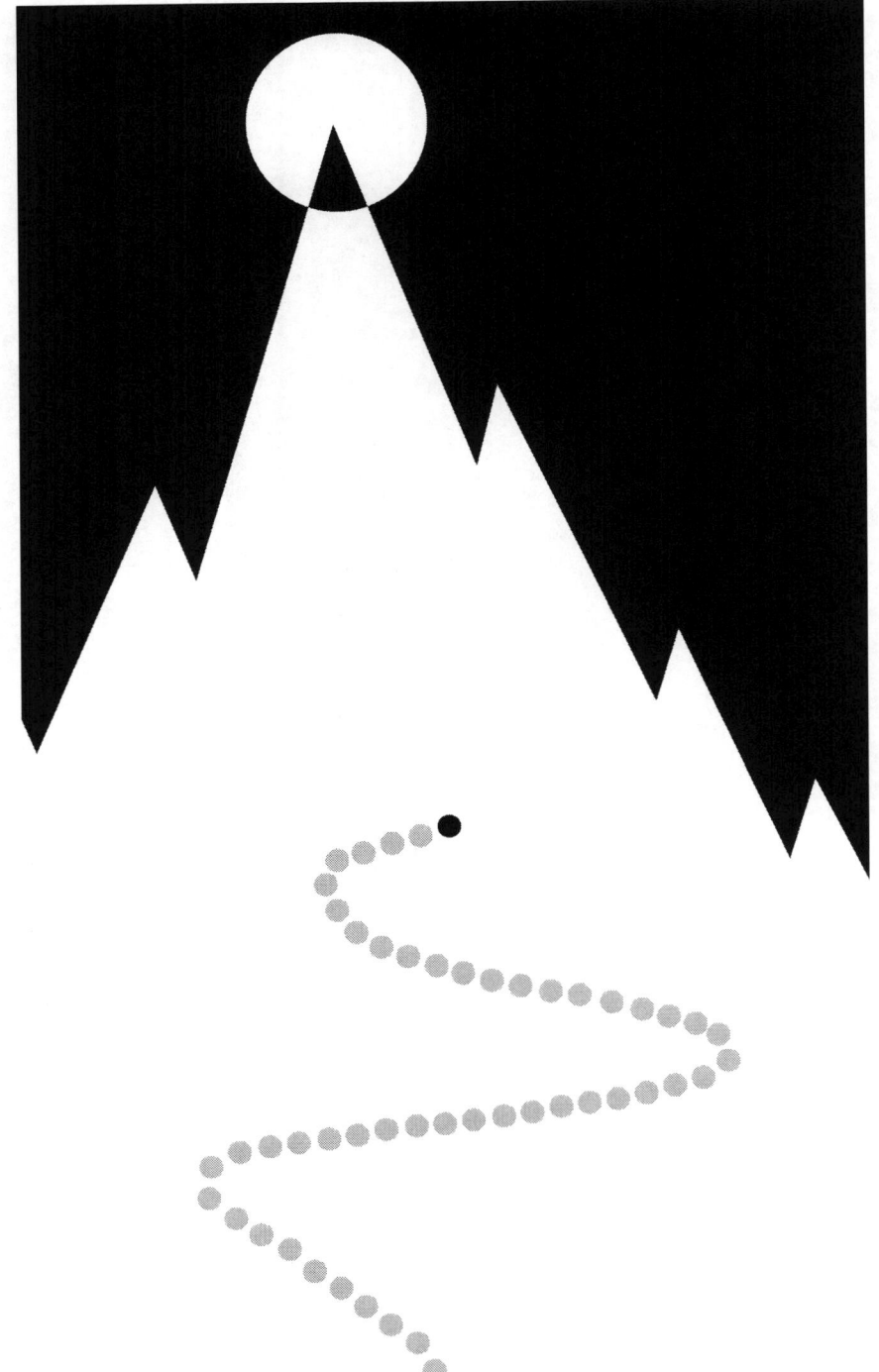

12
Is Christ Enough?
Exploring the Position Christ Holds in Our Lives.

He was a young man, but life was hard. He's been paralyzed from birth and life felt pretty hopeless. It was first century Palestine and there were essentially no social programs to help him out. Oh, there were family and friends who did what they could, maybe a little something from the Roman dole, but mainly he was forced to eke out a living by begging near the temple. He had four life-long friends. They were great guys, guys that really took him under their proverbial wings. They would help him out when they could and they carried him to the prime begging spots. He didn't know what life would be like without them. One day they came to him and said something about a rabbi who was in town. Evidently the rabbi, who's name was Jesus, had a healing ministry. His friends were all excited. He's wasn't sure any of this would do any good. He'd been like this for so long that he wondered if there was even a point, but they were so excited that he agreed to go.

It appears Jesus was ministering in someone's home and the place was packed. There were all sorts of people going in, most with one kind of sickness or another. Some were being carried in, others were limping in under their own power. A large corner of the room was filled with Pharisees and they didn't look happy. It doesn't look like they're sick or hurting, they were just doing what they always did, taking up space, getting in the way, and looking for trouble. The young man's friends got as far as the door and there they were forced to stop. There was no way in, the place was packed to the rafters. The man said, "Oh well, you tried, thanks guys, it's alright, I'll live." The friends turned from the door, but then they took an unexpected turn. They begin walking up the sloped ground of the hill into which the house was build. The man wondered what they were doing as they carried him out onto the roof. He was getting more and more concerned. "What are they doing?" he though. They started to pull the roof tiles away and they began to dig. They were making a hole in the roof. "Oh come on guys, stop! You're going get into trouble." It's true, the Roman soldiers were pretty tough on people who commit crimes and this was starting to feel like a crime.

When the hole was large enough they found some rope and tied their belts to the corners of the litter and began to lower the man through the hole.

Forgiven

Can you imagine the scene. Jesus was teaching to the literally packed house, when dust and debris began to fall and all of the sudden sunlight was shining through the now gaping hole in the roof. The crowd was abuzz at the spectacle. Slowly right in front of Jesus something began to descend through the hole. Before long it was apparent, a paralyzed man was being lowered through the hole, to the space before Jesus. I wonder how the young man felt. Was he embarrassed being at the center of this spectacle? The story I'm retelling is found in Mark 2:1-12. What's really fascinating is what happened next. It appears that when Jesus saw the man, He looked up through the hole in the roof and saw four friends looking down in eager expectation. Mark then writes, "When Jesus saw their faith..." and the question must be asked, "Whose faith?" It does not appear from the text that "their" included the man on the mat. It appears rather that the text refers to Jesus seeing the faith of the men who cared enough to dig a hole through a roof to get help for their friend. It was their faith that moved Jesus to action. It wasn't the faith of the man who needed healing that got this reaction, rather it was the faith of the ones who bore his stretcher.

Jesus looked the man in the eye and said, "Your sins are forgiven." and it is here that I get stuck. You see, this to me has always felt anticlimactic. This story sometimes makes me wonder if I am spiritual enough to do what I do. I keep feeling like, "It's great that the man's sins were forgiven, but Jesus, you know that's not really what he wanted." It's probably not what his friends wanted either. I'd have to imagine they were all there for a physical healing. He was carried in, but they were hoping he'd be walking out. When my thinking used to go in that direction, my next thought was the young man was lucky that the Pharisees were there. I'd like to tell the rest of the story from the man on the mat's point of view, as I imagine it.

"My sins are forgiven? That's great I suppose, but can He even do that?" I looked up at Jesus, wanting to ask for more, but I wasn't sure that I should. After all, how many sins could I have committed. I've been paralyzed for life. I have to be carried everywhere, How much trouble could I get into? There was something warm and compassionate in His eyes, but before I could speak, I saw He wasn't looking at me anymore. Instead He was looking at the Pharisees in the back of the room. I didn't hear them saying anything, but the look on their faces said it all. When He spoke it was almost as if he could hear what they were thinking. He looked right at them and said, ""Why are you thinking these things? Which is easier: to say to this paralyzed man, 'Your sins are forgiven,' or to say, 'Get up, take your mat and walk'? But I want you to know that the Son of Man has authority on earth to forgive sins."

Then he looked at me, right in the eyes, but where before they looked so soft and compassionate, now they were piercing and powerful. He said "I tell you take up your mat and go home." It was amazing, all of the sudden there was a warmth in my legs like I have never felt before. I would have said , "It felt like electric shocks," but electricity won't be discovered for 17 centuries so I'll just say "warm." When he said arise and walk, I thought and my legs moved. I pulled them under me and stood to my feet. He smiled at me and I took up my mat and for the first time in my life, I walked out the door and as I walked, everyone (well everyone but the Pharisees) was praising God.

That's where Mark ends the story, but is it okay if I go a little further? What I am about to share is not biblical, I am using my imagination informed by the Spirit and by human nature. We don't know this happened, but I think it's likely. So here's how I think the story ends.

"I couldn't believe it. I was walking. Jesus healed me. That Jesus is no mere Rabbi. There's something special about him." By the time I got out the door, my friends were there hugging me. They were jumping up and down. We were jumping up and down. Then one of the guys said, "C'mon dude." "Where are we going?" I said. He replied, "That roof ain't gonna fix itself." Yes my first action as a healed man was to patch a roof. "I didn't make the hole, why should I fix it?" I joked, but I was thrilled. For the first time in my life, I wasn't begging, I was working. That night they had a feast in my honor and I saw her. Oh my word she was beautiful. I had seen her many times, I always thought she was the most beautiful woman I'd ever seen. She was always kind and came up to me and talked to me on my litter. This was different. I could stand now, I could walk. I could look her in the eye. I could dance, Well I couldn't dance well, but I had the physical ability to dance. So I asked her to dance and I left her lead.

The next day I got a job. You'll find "miraculously healed" looks good on a resume. I got a job as a roofer. Now I could provide for myself and make a living. I began making up for lost time. Every time Rabbi Jesus was nearby, I would go to see Him. I became one of his followers. It made sense, He changed my life. Sometimes I would take Rebekah (that is her name) along to hear him and she started to believe as well. One night I asked her to marry me. We married and before long my first son was born. Things were not going well for Jesus. The Pharisees and Sadducees, all seemed to hate Him. I couldn't figure that out because the more I heard, the more I began to believe He might be the Messiah. Those old snakes could do what they want. I placed my trust in the One who healed me.

Then one day, they did what they wanted. They accused Him, they beat Him and they crucified Him. They put him to death. I saw him carry the cross and later I watched from a distance as they took Him down and placed Him in the tomb. I grieved bitterly. The One who saved me was dead. I owed Him so much. I would gladly have given Him my life, because He gave me life. I was with the 11 and the others in the upper room. I was scared, we all were, but all of the sudden Jesus entered the room. Walked right through the locked door, but He wasn't a ghost, He was solid. He was still human but somehow better. He ate with us and He taught us and He told us to wait for the Holy Spirit. He is risen. He is the Messiah. The one who healed me is the Messiah.

Well the years wore on, and the disciples were going everywhere spreading the Gospel and spreading the church. I kept on roofing and helping the church where I could. Rebekah and I had six more children, three more boys and three girls, and I raised them all to follow Jesus. Then one day when I was 80, my legs just didn't want to hold me anymore. I knew I was near the end and so I called my family to me. Sons and daughters, sons-in-law and daughters-in-law, grandchildren and more. I looked at that room full of people and realized all of them were in my life because of Jesus. There were tears but there was also joy. I was surrounded by love and the signs of a life well lived, and I closed my eyes in peace knowing they would open in a place beyond my wildest dreams and we would be together forever.

Why did I finish out the story? To show you a crucial point that might be easily overlooked. Do you remember the thoughts of disappointment when Jesus' reply to the man on the mat was that his sins were forgiven. That's probably not what he wanted. What he really wanted was to walk and Jesus made that so as well. When it happened, you probably thought, finally he got his miracle. What I want you to see though, was that while the physical healing was awesome, there came a time in the man's life when those healed legs failed again, this time forever. And while all the rest of the story was speculation, what you really need to know is that all of Jesus' physical healings and even the people that He raised from the dead, those miracles were temporary. Eventually the man from our story's time ran out for this world and when that happened, we ought to realize that the first miracle was the greater one. Physical healing is temporary, God's grace and forgiveness in Christ are what lead to eternal life. The work of Christ in our lives for forgiveness and salvation, is the greater miracle.

And all of this begs a question:

Is Christ enough? I can't answer that question for your heart. Only you know the position He holds in your life, but I can answer the question in general with a resounding yes. He paid the price we could not pay and if we place our trust and faith in Him, if we believe everything the Bible says about Him, and most importantly that we believe that what He did on the cross was done to pay the price for our sins, then we will live forever in His perfect love. Here on earth, we get to live to serve Him, to reflect the light of His love and grace into the dark corners of our world. We get to live here in this world on purpose, for a purpose, as His ambassadors and as His children and then when this life is done, when our time has run out, we get to go to the Heaven He prepared for us from before time began.

Don't miss this, what was broken in the garden is restored in heaven. The relationship that was broken is remade and the wall between us and God is torn down, once and for all. We, who have no righteousness of our own, get to enter heaven wrapped in the perfection of our perfect Savior, Jesus Christ. Jesus secured the eternity of all who would believe and I think that should show us, that Jesus Christ is more than enough.

13
His Grace is Enough
Exploring God's Amazing Grace

It was a terrible day, but as it goes with most bad days, this one went on to get much worse. I was the pastor of a church plant and things were not going well. About two years into the plant, I pushed myself so hard that I ended up in the hospital with a mild heart attack. As mentioned before, when it first happened I was very angry with God, but it actually ended up being a blessing in disguise. Through it, God showed me that everything was not up to me and that I needed to depend on Him and work at getting help. Once God helped me with those priorities, things started to improve for a little while.

I learned to get a little more rest here and there and I really started looking at the gifts of my folks. We even grew a little. We went from our starting seven people to about 31 and things were looking up. I even had a few people who were starting to look ready to move into leadership roles and provide my wife and I with some much needed assistance. A few of the folks made some choices I had to address and several of them left. I was devastated. Another person who had serious potential told me God told them they had to leave. It was just one thing after another and I started seeing this thing that I had devoted so much of my life to, falling apart. I was actually at a point of pretty profound grief.

I should also probably tell you that I have struggled with depression on and off for most of my life and even though I could see the good that happened in it, the heart attack had somewhat exacerbated that condition. To put it mildly, I was in a pit of despair, and then it got worse.

All of this stuff was going through my mind as I prepared to go out on my prayer walk. Before I did my walk each morning, I always tried to read Scripture. On this particular morning, I read 2 Corinthians 11. Let me tell you, if you're in any form of church leadership, and you're feeling at all inadequate, you know, like you'll never be enough, whatever you do, do not read 2 Corinthians 11. It will tear you up.

You see, 2 Corinthians 11 is where Paul starts boasting. Now even as he boasts, he confesses that he is talking like a fool. In this passage he confronts prideful people by showing them all the great stuff that God has done through Him. It would look like an extreme lack of humility, but what it really is, is Paul calling people to a better mind set and a better way.

He speaks of his pedigree as pharisee of pharisees and a Jew to the core. He speaks of having worked harder, been imprisoned for his faith more, having been beaten and flogged more severely. He relates being exposed to death over and over. He speaks of having been stoned and lashed, forty minus one (the Romans believed forty lashes would kill a man so in their "mercy" they held back one lash), beating one almost to death, but not quite. Paul had that five times. He was also shipwrecked three times and spent a day and a night in the open sea. He spoke of being in danger from virtually everyone, virtually everywhere, of being cold and naked and hungry and thirsty and still he persevered.

I was broken and hurting, feeling like maybe the worst, most incompetent minister of all time, when I read that passage. I was already questioning my call and my fitness for ministry when I read about "Super Paul, the endurance machine" and I felt pathetic. There's Paul enduring all these things, any one of which could have left him dead, but still he persevered. Meanwhile, I was falling apart over a few people who decided to leave my church. I felt like such a loser, but the passage was read and now it was time for my walk.

It took about thirty seconds for the tears to begin to flow. I live in the country and very few people were around to see my breakdown, which was probably a very good thing. I was not enough and I never would be. "I might as well quit." I was even starting to think maybe that was what God wanted I was at the end of my rope and I just wept.

In the church, comparison is deadly. Compare yourself to someone else and you will either come away feeling discouraged or prideful, and neither of those is helpful. If you're a church leader, there are hundreds of lessons in Scripture you can learn from Paul, but comparing yourself to him is a fool's errand. You're not likely to come up looking very good against the guy who wrote such a huge portion of the New Testament. I was coming up way short and I knew it and my plan was to finish this walk, go home and write my letter of resignation, I was done.

The thing is God was with me. I believe He is always close by and lives in our hearts, but on that day, His presence was thick and His mercy was thicker. I needed Him and He was there. I began to calm down, and the Lord began to remind me of Paul's thorn. Yes Paul did all that great stuff. Yes Paul stood His ground in the face of tremendous persecution. Was he tough? Yes, but not on His own. You see in the very next chapter Paul changes his tone in big ways. In chapter 12, Paul starts to talk about His thorn.

Paul's Thorn

What was the Thorn? We are never told. Scholars make various assumptions, like the problem was with Paul's eyes, an aftermath of his being temporarily blinded by Jesus on the road to Damascus, but there really isn't anything in scripture to confirm that. What we do know is, whatever it was, it was an immense bother to the man who endured everything that we read in chapter 11. As a matter of fact, the same man who survived all those things, begged God three times to take whatever this thorn was, away.

In chapter 12, Paul continues the boasting. It appears even he is not sure if what happened to him was actually a physical occurrence or just a vision, but it sure looks like God took Paul to Heaven, similar to what He did with John in the book of Revelation, and God taught Paul there. Yes, you read that right, if this passage is to be believed (and I believe it with all my heart), then Paul got his Christian seminary education at the feet of God Himself, in Heaven. Whether in a vision or in person, we're not sure, but nonetheless, this is extraordinary. Paul goes on to speak as if this vision or occurrence happened to someone else and says he will boast about that person, but not himself. I've often wondered why Paul chose to express himself in this way and the only conclusion I can come to is that the event was so transformative that he felt like a different person because of it.

While Paul does say he will not boast about himself, there is one exception. He says he will boast about his weaknesses. In my modern, American mindset this is definitely counter-cultural. We don't usually want to laud our weaknesses, we bury our weaknesses and talk about our strengths. Why? Because our weaknesses are those areas where we feel insufficient—where we feel like we're not enough. This takes me back to my prayer walk on that fateful day.

I never pictured my church plant ending up this way. I figured, to quote one of my favorite movies, "If you build it, they will come." I saw this thing on an upward trajectory. We would grow and grow and grow and the sky was the limit. I would succeed where others had failed. I would do church different. I would do it right and the multitudes would come. That we would struggle and fail had rarely even crossed my mind, but on that day, the thought didn't just cross, it moved to the middle of my mind and stayed there. I was a failure and a loser and I would never be anything. My church had become just another in a long list of failed attempts. Depression does that, but God's grace was about to fall upon me.

As I was drawn to the thorn, I began to get it. The mighty Paul had his own source of pain, and while it seemed minor compared to all the other things that Paul had endured, this was the thing that made him cry "uncle." This was the chink in the armor. This was the weakness and I was so glad he decided to boast about it.

It's important to consider why Paul had the thorn. First of all he calls it a messenger of Satan, designed to torment him for the purpose of keeping him from being conceited. I can relate. Had things come through the way I thought they would have, it would have been pretty easy to begin claiming credit for what God had done and that is not humility, that's pride. Paul's thorn kept him from pride, was my thorn keeping me my pride from undoing me, as well?

Paul speaks of begging God to take the thorn away. Whatever it was, it was unbearable to him. Three times he begged. Three times God said, in effect, "No!" Well what he actually said was "My grace is sufficient for you, for my power is made perfect in weakness." (2 Corinthians 12:9 NIV) His grace is sufficient. His grace is enough. He won't remove the thorn. That would pave the way for conceit in Paul's life. Instead the thorn would be a reminder and God would give Paul the grace to stand up under it. It's not everything that Paul wanted, but it would be enough. This is what we need to see. I began to think about how many times I've asked God to take away my penchant to go to the dark side of depression and how at times, even today, it still remains. It's better but it remains. Could this be my thorn? See I didn't want to dwell in my weakness. I wanted to live in strength. I wanted God to make me strong, but if I am strong, then will I be strong enough? Will I be sufficient in my own strength and if I am sufficient in my own strength, will I need God? Of course I will, but will I see the need or will I be blinded by success that isn't even truly mine to claim.

The rest of verse 9 says "Therefore I will boast all the more gladly about my weaknesses, so that Christ's power may rest on me." I don't ever want to be insufficient to the task before me. I always want to be more than enough, but if I'm always sufficient in myself, I will never get to see that God is enough. The things I can do in my own power do not allow me to depend on the power of God. When, instead, He gives grace to endure, I can see that His grace as enough. I can still bring everything I have to the table, but I can see the power of God come in and do everything I can't. He has the power and He gets the glory.

Paul finishes his thought by saying in verse 10, "That is why, for Christ's sake, I delight in weaknesses, in insults, in hardships, in persecutions, in difficulties. For when I am weak, then I am strong." When I am weak, then I am strong? It almost sounds nonsensical doesn't it? It isn't. When His grace is enough, we have no choice but to rely on His strength. Paul knew this and so He could delight in His weaknesses and look at how God worked in those weaknesses. Paul took the church to the halls of power and to the ends of the earth. Paul recorded some of the greatest wisdom in all of Scripture. Paul did mighty things in his weaknesses, because in his weakness, God was strong. In Paul's life, God's grace was enough. Is it enough for you?

It would be great if God bailed us out of every pain, and that's what we all want, most of the time, but that's not always how this works. You see we all ultimately want to be independent, but what God wants is for us to realize that we are totally dependent on Him and interdependent on each other. That we would live in relationship with Him and with our brothers and sisters. As such, we need our strengths and He gives those in abundance, but we also need our weaknesses, because we cannot learn to depend on God unless we have to depend on God. His strength is made perfect in our weaknesses, so He doesn't pull us out of them, He simply walks with us through them. His grace is indeed enough for us.

As I began to consider Paul's thorn that day, I began to wonder about my own thorn. Could it be that depression is my thorn? Could this be a weakness that God could turn into a strength? I think it can. As a matter of fact, I think it has been. Believe me when I tell you, He can still take it away any time He wants, but in the mean time, His grace is enough. It is that grace that has made me compassionate to the suffering and struggling. This is vital in the work God has called me to. It is God's grace that makes me able to see what's happening in the midst of a trial and to look forward in hope, rather than wallowing in despair. His grace seems to constantly remind me of Romans 8:28 (NIV). "In ALL things (emphasis mine) God works for the good of those who love Him, who have been called according to His purpose." This much I know, I love God and He loves me. Despite the way I felt on that day, I know I am called according to His purpose, and if that's the case, then I can look at every trial and seek out the way that it can work to my good. His grace is for me and it is enough. My thorn will not overcome me, because God has given me the grace to endure.

There was one other thing that came to me on that day, in the midst of all this thought on thorns. In my mind's eye, I began to see Jesus, as he was being led to Golgotha. On His head was a brutal crown of thorns—long sharp thorns goring His flesh and causing even more indescribable pain. Since I have been a believer, I have known that Jesus bore my sins as He went to the cross, but this image begged a question. Did He also bear my thorns?

His grace is enough. Is it enough for you?

147

14

Is God Enough?
Exploring God's Sovereignty and Sufficiency

So often we Christians look at Christ as first and foremost but there are two other "people" that compose the Trinity, God the Father and God the Holy Spirit, yet needless to say they are all of tremendous importance. After all when Jesus walked the earth, He lived in perfect submission and obedience to the Father, prayed to the Father, was sent by the Father and when He ascended, He returned to the Father. Today He intercedes for us before the Father. When Jesus returned to the Father, He sent the Holy Spirit to live in all believers, to guide us and teach us and even to pray for us when we don't know what to pray. All three persons of the Trinity make up the one God who we worship. He is one God in three persons which is, in some ways, extremely confusing, and I doubt I will be able to alleviate your confusion here, except to say, in those three persons, He is over us, beside us and in us, and as such we are never alone, never without help and never abandoned. Because of this He is all that we will ever need. He is more than enough.

So let's start by looking at the Father. We meet the Father in the fourth word of the Bible. "In the beginning God..." Translation, God has always existed, and with Him, the Son and the Holy Spirit. It's kind of cool if you think about it. I have stressed several times in this volume that God is all about relationships, but if you think about it, He is also in a way a relationship unto Himself. We'll get back to this later, but for now suffice it to say there was never a time when God wasn't. He has no Creator. He has no beginning. He has no end. He is infinite and He is capable of anything good. Nothing good is beyond His power. He is the very definition of enough, and He supersedes enough, infinitely.

In the fifth word of Scripture we learn about one of God's primary attributes. "In the beginning, God created..." God is Creator. He created all there is, and it is here that we need to spend some time. One of the things I love is that God creates and then He gave us, as His children, the ability to create. The reason I love this so much probably has something to do with the fact that I love to create. Of course we create differently. When I want to create, the first thing I need to do is go to an art supply store and get all the materials I need to do the project at hand. God doesn't create that way. God creates *ex nihilo* which is a Latin phrase, meaning "from nothing." God can create something from nothing. God speaks and things come into existence. The other way that God creates is differently from us, is we can make beautiful things, things that boggle the imagination. God does too, but God also makes His creations live. Let's go back to Genesis 1 and explore Gods creative process in progress.

Frame of Reference

Now before I go on, I need to tell you about the perspective I'm taking. I know there are many theories on how the earth and its inhabitants came into existence and I know tremendous struggle and debate has come as to which is the actual path. For our purposes, I am going to take a literal approach, taking the account of Genesis 1 as the eyewitness account of the only One who was there as it happened. If this is oversimplified, so be it. This is how it says it happened in God's Word. The scientists can sort out the details and they will from here to eternity, probably quite literally. That's okay, God gave them their inquisitive minds, to learn these things and help us to understand all that God has given us, but for our purposes, we're simply going to take God at His Word.

"In the beginning, God created the heavens and the earth." It goes on to speak of how the earth was formless and empty, covered with water and in total darkness. This is the very beginning stage— God at the raw materials stage of creating.

He has just started the process with a water covered blob of material. It also says that His Spirit, was hovering over the waters. As any good creative would do, God turns on the light. He says let there be light and there was light. This, once again, shows us God's pattern of creation. God speaks and things happen. Oh that we would remember this as we live our lives and obey when God speaks, but that's free will and I'm getting ahead of myself. God speaks light into existence. The next thing that happens establishes a pattern for the rest of the days of creation. When God sees the light, He says it is good. When God sees most everything He made, He says it is good. This should not be surprising. God is perfect and so was His creation, as it was originally created. Everything God makes is good. Everything God makes works and God makes everything work.

Day One

On the first day after God made light, He separated the light from the darkness. He made day and night on that first day. Now as we continue through the process, it is vital that we consider God's omniscience. God knows everything. He can see the chain of events past, present and future from the beginning. He knows everything that can and will happen and all the ramifications of every choice. He truly begins with the end in mind. For the purpose of creation, God already knows the finished project before He starts the work, He already knows the purpose of everything He is doing. He knows what the earth will be and who and what will inhabit it, before the work begins (not to mention the entire story arc of all history) and He creates accordingly.

Day Two

On the second day of creation, God took some of the water that was on the earth and put it above the earth and He called the space in-between the waters "sky." Now I know there are some who will want to balk at this. There's no water above the earth. If you're thinking that, consider this question: What color is the sky? Whenever I ask this question, most people will say, "blue." Most people are wrong. The sky is not blue. Think about it, everything above the surface of the earth is sky. If the sky were blue, the only thing you would see would be some gaseous blue cloud everywhere, all the time. No, the sky is transparent, so why does it look blue? Well sunlight (I know we haven't gotten to the sun yet but please bear with me) bounces off the water vapor in the sky and it reflects blue light back to our eyes, hence there is water above the earth, just like God said. Of course the other reason we know there is water up there is because sometimes it comes down. This too is part of God's design because there will be a time when the earth will need a good watering, but again I am getting ahead of myself. The creation of the sky, the atmosphere, is the second day,

Day Three

On the third day, life begins. First God pushes back the waters so that the dry land can appear. Now there is land and sea. Remember, God knows exactly what He is going to create and how it is all going to work. He creates land and sea so that creatures can inhabit them. He knows how all the chemical processes and all the complexities of life on earth and He creates accordingly. He knows that when these creatures come about they are going to breathe in oxygen, but their biological processes are going to make it that they breathe something different out. The air they breath out will be, in a sense. polluted with carbon, making carbon dioxide (yes scientists, I am fully aware that I am oversimplifying the process). Well eventually an atmosphere of carbon dioxide will not sustain life on the earth, so God creates a kind of filtering system. He creates something that can take in carbon dioxide, utilize the carbon and put out oxygen again. This filtering system is called plant life and God made a vast array of different kinds, all with the ability to reproduce in kind and fill the earth. Of course the plant life had a secondary function. The plants were also created to supply the eventual creatures with the food God knew they would need. Again God looked at what He created and said it was good, because everything God makes works and God makes everything work.

Day Four

Day four is interesting and confusing at the same time. You see on day four, God made the sun, the moon and all the stars. About now I can see someone raising their hand with a question. "I thought you said God said 'Let there be light' on day one, but now you're telling me He only made the sources of light on day four. If that's so where did the light come from on days one through three?" Well I'm glad you asked, the answer is found in 1 John 1:5 where it says "God is light, in Him there is no darkness at all." Before the sources of light were created, God was the source the light. The Bible also tells us that in the "New heaven and the new earth" described in Revelation 21 (specifically verse 23) that God will once again be the source of light, but for now we have the sun, the moon and all the stars, to regulate day and night and seasons and years, with the stars to guide us around this world (I'm getting ahead of myself again). Here's where it gets fascinating.

The sun looks like a little glowing ball in the sky. Of course we know this is not the case. The sun is actually many times larger than the earth and immensely hot. The reason it looks so small is because it is 93,000,000 miles away. It's a good thing too, because if we were any closer, life as we know it could not be sustained on earth because it would be too hot. If we were any farther away, we would freeze. God keeps us at just the right distance from the sun, all the time, making the earth able to sustain life, because everything God makes works and God makes everything work.

Now I have a weird mind sometimes. I had this feeling that people probably could not understand how far 93,000,000 miles is, so I had to come up with an illustration, an impossible illustration, but an illustration nonetheless. So imagine we could build a bridge from the earth to the sun. It's a physical impossibility, of course, but imagine it. Now imagine you wanted to drive to the sun. You would get into your massively heat shielded car and begin to drive. Suppose you drove your car at a whopping 100 miles per hour. If you drove that fast and you never stopped, to eat, sleep, refuel or go to the bathroom, it would take you 107 years to drive to the sun. God's creation is amazing, but let's go further.

Has anyone ever looked at you and said, "Will you just sit still?" Do you realize the most correct answer is "I can't?" You have never, ever sat still for even one second in your entire life. As a matter of fact you are currently on the most amazing thrill ride in the universe and you don't even know it. Right now, even if you're sitting completely motionless, by virtue of being on the surface of the earth, you are spinning at 1,000 miles per hour. You also probably think you're sitting on a nice level floor, but that's also not true, You're sitting on the side of a 25,000 mile circumference ball. The reason you don't falloff is because that ball is spinning at the aforementioned 1,000 miles per hour, but it gets better. The earth is also revolving around the sun at a speed of 64,000 miles an hour and you don't even know it, because because everything God makes works and God makes everything work.

Do you realize you travel over 500,000,000 miles every year of your life, and I haven't even taken into account that the sun is also revolving in a much larger orbit. No wonder you're tired sometimes. God made all of these amazing things happen to sustain life on this planet and we're only up to day four, but once again when God saw what He made, He said it was good.

Day Five
On day five, God began to show off. Okay, I have to stop there. God is perfect and sinless, so I'm not sure it's possible

for Him to show off. (Is showing off a sin?) But the things He created on day five are so amazing that it is hard to imagine it in any other way. You see it was on day five that God created the birds and the fish, some of his most amazing creatures. I mean consider the birds. Some of God's most amazingly beautiful creatures are birds. He made them bright and colorful, sometimes with color changing iridescent feathers. He made everything from the hummingbird to the ostrich, but it wasn't enough to make such a wide array of beauty, He also made them (well most of them) able to fly. They're remarkable in every way, perfectly flawless in design. but that wasn't enough. He also made the fish. from the tiniest tetra to the gigantic whale shark, all able to exist below the surface of the deep, in every shape and size and color, some able to withstand tremendous pressures. He made fish for the deepest, darkest parts of the ocean, that have within them their own sources of light. He even made a fish that is electric. He made all these amazing creatures, every one a work of art in appearance, form and function, all designed to balance each other out and to sustain what God had made, and when God saw what He had made, He said it was good.

Day Six

As we come to day six, the land animals come into being, and again a wide array of balanced creation. From the smallest gnat, to the largest elephant, all sorts of amazing creatures populate the land. Some of those creatures will eat the plants, others will feed on other animals and there is a circle of life that permeates through all of it. There is also incredible design. For example, have you ever noticed that male birds are predominantly beautiful, while female birds tend toward drabness. Males are virtually every color in the rainbow while female birds mostly stick to the tertiary colors, browns and grays. There is a reason for that. Male birds have one primary purpose—to attract a mate and perpetuate the species. The female birds, as a rule, do almost everything else. They need to sit on the eggs and keep them warm so they'll hatch. They have to protect the nest from predators and so God created them to blend in. They are in effect camouflaged.

God made some animals to stand out, while others blend in. He made some animals look like other things, so they can hide in plain sight. He made some animals look like other animals to make them able to scare their predators away. He even made a few species that can change colors. to blend into their surroundings. God made some animals who don't have to blend in at all. An example of this is the poison dart frog. Found in the Amazon rain forest, they are some of the most beautiful, brightly colored animals there are. They couldn't blend in if they tried but they don't have to because they are some of the most deadly poisonous animals on earth. Get some of the mucous from their skin in an open cut and you don't have long to live. That's how they got their name, The indigenous people of the Amazon figured out how to weaponize them. What's even more amazing is that if they are deprived of one particular bug they eat, they cease to be poisonous, or at least cease to be as poisonous. To keep their populations from exploding, God made an animal called the Fire Bellied Snake that can eat them, because something in the snake's saliva neutralizes the poison. Once again, God made everything work and everything God makes works.

God's design permeates every element of animal life. For example did you ever look at a deer or a rabbit or virtually any of the prey animals? Did you ever notice the position of their eyes? Plant eating animals usually have their eyes on the sides of their heads rather than on the front. The reason for this is simple. While they are eating they need to be able to keep an eye out for what eats them. Contrastingly, predators tend to have their eyes on the fronts of their heads because everything they eat is running away. Speaking of which, your eyes are on the front of your head, so enjoy your hamburger, in moderation of course.

Then there are some animals who are just mind-blowing. Take for example the bombardier beetle. There is a species of the bombardier beetle on every continent except Antarctica. They come in a variety of colors, but what makes them unique is not what's happening on the outside but rather what happens on the inside. The bombardier beetle has a very unique defense mechanism within his body. In the beetle's abdomen there are two sacs. One of those sacs contains a chemical called hydroquinone. Hydroquinone is a chemical often used in cosmetics. The other sac holds a more familiar chemical, hydrogen peroxide, a chemical commonly used to clean wounds. The household version of this chemical is found in a very diluted form. In its less diluted form it can be used as rocket fuel. These chemicals on their own are not necessarily harmful, but mix them together and they explode and that's what happens inside the bombardier beetle. No the beetle himself does not explode, but when the bombardier beetle senses a threat, those two sacs begin to contract, to squeeze, and they squeeze the chemicals into a third organ in their body where they mix, shooting boiling hot liquid out the bug's (there's no nice way to say this) butt. I've seen video of a large spider coming up on one of these beetles, thinking he's about to have an easy meal when all of the sudden there's a flash and the spider runs away as fast as his eight legs will carry him. You'd run too if you just got shot in the face by boiling hot bug juice.

Enter the Masterpiece

Think this through. if God put all this amazing detail into one little bug, imagine the care He put into everything else. Everything God makes works, and God makes everything work. About now you might be wondering why I spent all that time talking about the creation of the universe in a book that is about being enough? I did it because we're only halfway through day six. In the last half of day six, God seems to change up how He works. For the most part through the first five days, God speaks things into existence, but around the middle of day six, God changes the way He does things. Where before He spoke, now He sculpts. He puts His divine hands into the dust of the earth and starts to sculpt. He's not just making animals here, He's making a masterpiece and a monument. You see this last creation is not like the rest. This last creation was made to look like Him, in His image, and when He was satisfied with His creation, He breathed His own life into it and it became a living soul. It was different from all the other creations. It was made for immortality. It was made for eternity. It was made to be the object of God's love, and it was made to love God in return. It was made to represent God and it was made to dwell with God. It was our first parents. It was humanity. It was you. You were made to love God and to be loved by God and you are loved by God. If you still question if you're enough, think about that.

Now I'm not saying you're perfect, and I'm not saying you're not broken. I can't say that about myself either, but you are still the object of God's perfect divine love, so the question of the chapter remains, Is God enough... for you? The Creator of all there is, the one who made everything work, loves you and has a plan for you that ends at the glorious beginning of an eternity in a place of perfect love and peace forever. That should be more than enough.

I know what you want to say, "That's great for some day, but I live here and now, and this world is hard and cold. God may have made it good, but it's not good now. Right now I need help and I don't feel like I'm up to it." The good news is, He has not left you alone.

Is the Holy Spirit Enough?

Just before Jesus died on the cross, as recorded in the book of John, He was preparing His disciples for his coming death. In John 16:5, 6 (NIV) He said "but now I am going to him who sent me. None of you asks me, 'Where are you going?' Rather, you are filled with grief because I have said these things." It's true. These people had spent the last three years with Jesus. He taught them. He guided them. They went through good times and bad times together and they loved each other. Now He was going to die at the hands of the very people He came to save. Of course the disciples didn't understand what all that meant. They just knew their friend was about to suffer and die. They probably also wondered what that meant for them and they were grieving. They needed some good news.

Jesus gave it to them. Even though He was leaving, they would not be alone. "But very truly I tell you, it is for your good that I am going away. Unless I go away, the Advocate will not come to you; but if I go, I will send him to you." (John 16:7 NIV) The Advocate Jesus is speaking of is the Holy Spirit, the third person of the Trinity, God the Spirit would live in them. They no doubt would have known about the Holy Spirit. Throughout the Old Testament there were many times where the Holy Spirit would come upon a person to give them supernatural power to accomplish a task for the Lord, and then the Spirit would return to the Father. This would be different. When Jesus sent the Holy Spirit, the Spirit would indwell all who believe, forever. Wherever they went, God the Spirit would be with them, empowering them to live out God's plan for their lives. That promise was not just for twelve guys in the first century. It is a promise for every man, woman and child who receives Jesus a Lord and Savior. In other words, the Holy Spirit is for you. This is incredibly good news. If you have received Jesus as Lord and Savior, His Spirit is within you. So what is the role of the Spirit?

Your Friend, Conviction

Well, Jesus tells us. "When he comes, he will prove the world to be in the wrong about sin and righteousness and judgment: about sin, because people do not believe in me; about righteousness, because I am going to the Father, where you can see me no longer; and about judgment, because the prince of this world now stands condemned." (John 16:8-11 NIV) Simply put, the Holy Spirit will convict of us of our sins. "Convict" may seem like a strong word, conjuring images of prison cells, but that's not where this is going. Conviction is actually your friend. It helps you to see when you're going in the wrong direction, so you can turn around. This act of turning around is also called repentance. The Spirit also helps us to hold onto faith and belief when the hard times come. The Spirit helps us to be righteous which simply means to be more like God and living in a way that honors Him. Finally, He helps us see the plans of the condemned prince of this world (another name for Satan) and helps us to avoid the pitfalls he puts into our lives.

Continuing on Jesus tells us, "But when he, the Spirit of truth, comes, he will guide you into all the truth. He will not speak on his own; he will speak only what he hears, and he will tell you what is yet to come. He will glorify me because it is from me that he will receive what he will make known to you. All that belongs to the Father is mine. That is why I said the Spirit will receive from me what he will make known to you." (John 16:13-15 NIV) The Spirit becomes the voice of truth in our lives. He is, after all, part of the Trinity with Jesus, who said, "[I am] the truth…" God is truth and His Spirit guides us to truth. Further, the Spirit speaks only the Words of God into our lives. The Spirit glorifies God and helps us to do the same. What the Spirit received from God He makes known to us. He helps us and guides us.

Further in John 14:25-26 (NIV) Jesus tells us, "All this I have spoken while still with you. But the Advocate, the Holy Spirit, whom the Father will send in my name, will teach you all things and will remind you of everything I have said to you." He is our teacher and our guide and He keeps Jesus' teachings first and foremost in our hearts, which is exactly where they need to be if we are going to live this life, following God.

Paul reminds us in Romans 8:26-27 (NIV) "In the same way, the Spirit helps us in our weakness. We do not know what we ought to pray for, but the Spirit himself intercedes for us through wordless groans. And he who searches our hearts knows the mind of the Spirit, because the Spirit intercedes for God's people in accordance with the will of God." The Spirit gives strength in our weakness, prays for us when we are confused and don't know how to pray. He searches our hearts, and helps us.

Finally, looking all the way back to the birth story of Jesus, in Matthew 1:23 (NIV) we see "The virgin will conceive and give birth to a son, and they will call him Immanuel" (which means "God with us"). This is, in fact, what the incarnation of Jesus did. When Jesus walked the earth, He was God with us. Through the Holy Spirit, He still is. He lives with and in every believer, doing all the things listed above and more. Think about what that means, God quite literally lives in you, teaching you, empowering you and showing you the way.

Simply put, with the Holy Spirit, we are empowered for mission, and in Him we are up to the challenge. God is enough and He makes us enough.

15
Jesus Paid Enough
Exploring Salvation Through Christ

Ultimately, this is where we become enough. There is a debt that we all owe. It is the debt of our sin to a perfect God. The price is higher than we could ever pay and because of that debt we would all be lost and condemned forever, but all the way back in the beginning, God created us to love us and to be in relationship with us. That is still God's ultimate desire because of His great love for us, and so God made a plan to set us free from our sins forever. He sent His Son, Jesus to die in our place. Why this had to be is complicated but let's look into it briefly.

First off, God is completely fair and just. He is completely good. He means what He says and says what He means. He is perfect. He made covenants with humanity from the beginning. A covenant is like a contract, and one by one, we humans broke them all. Well not only is God perfect, but His Heaven is perfect. If we entered that Heaven in our imperfect state, Heaven would no longer be perfect. It would soon contain the same mess we have here on earth. Perfection and imperfection simply do not mix. So in order to enter Heaven, we who are imperfect need to be made perfect. We who are imperfect need a sacrifice to make atonement for us and make us perfect. Theologians call this "substitutionary atonement." The Bible says "The wages of sin is death…" (Romans 6:23A NIV) This cannot change, sin demands a sacrifice. The price to be paid for those sins is a perfect life, so none of us can be our own sacrifice. We need a perfect substitute. The rest of Romans 6:23 (NIV) gives the answer "…but the gift of God is eternal life in Christ Jesus our Lord."

Jesus fulfilled over 300 biblical prophecies. It is clear from this that He is exactly who He says He is. Jesus is the Son of

God, who came to lay down His life as a ransom for many. I know I have touched on this several times throughout this book, but please understand, Jesus' life, death and resurrection is ultimately what makes us enough. Placing our faith and trust in Him and what He has done for us is what brings us to eternal life and that faith is the only thing that can. We can't be good enough on our own. We need Jesus. Remember Jesus said, "I am the way and the truth and the life, no one comes to the Father, except through me." (John 14:6 NIV) If we want to get to eternal life, the only way is through Jesus. Jesus makes us enough.

Your Life Is a Line...

In this world we all face temptation and we all fall to that temptation and when we do, we fall into sin. I have long looked for a way to illustrate this and I think I have found it. I know you've seen those commercials. There's a closeup of a person, you can usually see no more than his or her head and shoulders. All of the sudden there appears an angel on one shoulder and a demon on the other. The demon starts off trying to tempt the person to indulge in something, usually some decadent dessert, and the angel tries to talk them out of it and maybe not coincidently, it usually seems like the angel loses out. Now these commercials are generally humorous, at least to some degree, but they are taking this way too lightly. Temptation is very real and it's a huge battle, not between two little imps on your shoulders, but between the two most powerful forces in the universe. The battle is for your soul. Your life is a line.

When I demonstrate this, I set up two easels on the far ends of a stage. On one end of that line is a portrait of Jesus, on the other a portrait of Satan, because ultimately that's the battle. Jesus is on one end and Satan is on the other. On one side is love, on the other, hate. On one side is life, on the other, death. On one side is light, on the other, darkness. You get the idea, polar opposites battling over you. You are somewhere in the middle, somewhere on the line between the two and faced with a choice.

Satan begins to do what he does best. I don't ever like to give him any praise of any kind, but there is something I must concede. He is good at what he does and what he does is tries to lure us into temptation. He knows just where to hit us and what to dangle in front of us to get us to turn toward him. We see the temptation, and too often we are off to the races, running headlong toward our own destruction. Remember that's his ultimate goal. His end is secure. He is headed to eternal destruction. The only thing he has left is to try to destroy what God loves most, and what God loves most is you. He tries to lure you to your destruction. Now if you already belong to Jesus, your ultimate destruction is off the table, but He will still try to destroy your witness, so that others won't see your life and leave the path to destruction. Before we go any further look at the picture below, look at the man and his position on the line. Look at the direction of his body. In order to turn toward temptation, in order to turn toward sin, do you see what he has to do? Yes, he has to turn his back on God and that is precisely what happens. When we turn toward sin, we are turning our backs on God, and we are ultimately turning toward our ruin, every time, all the time, no exceptions.

Now let's suppose you're on the dead sprint to death, heading to your own destruction, when suddenly you hear a little voice. The still small voice of God, of the Holy Spirit and He's saying, "Please stop. You're not going to like where this ends. It's painful. It's going to hurt a lot. I have something better for you. I love you." You hear that voice, and you hit the brakes and in that moment you turn around. You turn your back on sin and you turn to Jesus. That act is what we call repentance. Jesus gave His life to buy us that privilege, the privilege to turn around and turn to Him and to be rescued.

The Price Is Paid

Jesus died a horrible, painful death for us. Before the crucifixion, he was beaten almost to death, flogged with lead tipped whips, tearing his flesh and causing unspeakable pain. He was then forced to carry His cross through the streets and the mocking crowds until He fell under it's weight. The beating was too severe, someone else had to carry the cross the rest of the way. When He got to the place of crucifixion, they stripped Him and nailed Him to the cross. Then they raised the cross and dropped it's base into the hole prepared for it, jarring his whole body and likely dislocating His joints for even more pain. It was barbaric.

Before we go any further, we need to remember something. Jesus didn't have to do any of this. He had no guilt to deserve this sentence. He was literally and completely sinless, the only One in all history to live a sinless life. He was not just a man, He was the eternal son of God. Consider this for a moment. Jesus never sinned, but God put our sin on Him. 1 Corinthians 5:21 says, "God made him who had no sin to be sin for us, so that in him we might become the righteousness of God." This is the transaction. Jesus took all the sins of humanity, past, present and future upon Himself. He would be our sacrifice, our sin bearer. He took our cross, but it's even more. Before the crucifixion in the Garden of Gethsemane, Jesus was suffering. His anguish was so extreme that His body began to sweat drops of blood. A lot of people think that was because He knew the physical pain He was going to endure, and I believe He did, but I don't think that was the ultimate issue. Keep in mind Jesus is eternal. He existed long before He was born a human. He has been with the Father for all eternity. Consider also that sin separates us from God. In taking on our sin, this would be the first time that Jesus would be separated from God in all of eternity. That's what He did for us as He hung on that cross.

Crucifixion

Most people think that death by crucifixion was from the nails. That's simply not the case. Death by crucifixion is largely death by suffocation. The horrendous beatings and the shock to the system that it was, helped the process along. Many people never made it to the cross, they died in the flogging. When it came to crucifixion, the Romans were expert executioners. If they wanted to kill a person quickly they would just drive one nail through the person's both hands and let them hang from it. Hanging in that way, they couldn't expand their chest to get air into their lungs and they would die quickly. If the Romans wanted a person to suffer, they would crucify him as they did Jesus, arms stretched out to the sides with knees slightly bent and a nail through the feet. That way the person's survival instinct would kick in and they would push up against the nail through their feet in order to be able to breathe. They could live like that for days. It was horrible. That is the price our Savior paid. A high price so we could be enough.

167

The other thing you have to remember is Jesus knew what He was doing and He was in control of it all. When He was arrested, His disciples tried to fight to rescue Him. It's ironic if you think about it, If they had saved Him, He could not have saved them. He said as much to them when He said. "Put your sword back in its place," Jesus said to him, "for all who draw the sword will die by the sword. Do you think I cannot call on my Father, and he will at once put at my disposal more than twelve legions of angels? But how then would the Scriptures be fulfilled that say it must happen in this way?" (Matthew 26:52-54 NIV) Jesus knew this was the way it had to be, and He determined to pay the price. He also said, "The reason my Father loves me is that I lay down my life—only to take it up again. No one takes it from me, but I lay it down of my own accord. I have authority to lay it down and authority to take it up again. This command I received from my Father." (John 10:17-18 NIV) Jesus is no victim. He is the victor. His life was the price for victory, He would lay it down but God gave him the power to take it up again.

In John 19:30 (NIV) at the very end of His earthly life, He shouted out three words in a loud voice, "It is finished." and then note what it says next. "With that, he bowed his head and *gave up* his spirit." That is not a life taken, that is a life laid down and again it shows Jesus' ultimate control over the situation, but let's go back to his last three words. "It is finished." Now what I am about to say next will be shocking to some of you, so you may want to prepare yourself. Jesus Christ did not...

...speak English.

Yes, I know He does in most of the movies, but remember those are movies. In real life, Jesus predominantly spoke a language called Aramaic, so he did not actually say "It is finished." What He said was an Aramaic word that means "It is finished." The word He actually spoke was probably "tetellestai." and yes, it does mean "It is finished" but it also has a secondary meaning. It was a phrase used in the marketplace. When you had purchased something in those days before cash registers and receipts, you would give your money, the shopkeeper would give you your item and he or she would shout out, "tetellestai." It means "It is finished" but it also means, "Paid in full!" and that is exactly what Jesus did. He paid your sin debt in full. When He said, "It is finished." He wasn't talking about his life, as we'll see in a couple of days when He was raised from the dead. No, Jesus was talking about God's plan for salvation. All that needed to happen had happened. The price was paid. The Old Covenant of the law was fulfilled and the new covenant in Jesus' blood was here. From that time forward, all who believe in Jesus would be saved.

Jesus paid the price. Jesus paid enough. And when He paid your price, He made you enough. Receive His gift of salvation and Let Him make you enough today.

16
Am I Good Enough? Part 2
Exploring God's Will

As we near the end of this book, I wonder where you are today. Are you still discouraged? Have I written something that will make you think you're not good enough. Well you need to know, no matter where you are, you're good enough to start. They say a journey of a thousand miles begins with a single step. Maybe today is the day to take that first step.

Are you doubting because of something you have done, or maybe something you're continuing to do? Maybe today is the day to turn around and turn to Jesus. Give your sin to Him. He has already taken it to the cross. Ask Him to forgive you and ask Him to help you leave your sin there at the foot of the cross and never take it up again.

Are you wondering if you're enough because you don't compare to someone else. The answer to that is simple, stop comparing yourself to other people. They are on their journey and you are on yours, and while, for believers, all of our journeys end up in the same place, Heaven, the paths between here and there are varied and different. Instead, compare yourself to Jesus. Make no mistake, if you do, you will come up lacking. He's perfect, you're not, but He is the best example you can follow. Better than any example this world has to offer. So many people struggle with the will of God and what it is for their lives. The first thing to consider is totally biblical but not found in the Bible. It's found in something called the *Westminster Catechism*. It says, "The chief end of man is to glorify God and enjoy Him forever." We glorify God when we do our best in Him to honor Him in whatever He puts before us, pointing people to Him as the source of our strength and goodness. We give Him glory when we live to honor Him.

And finally if you want to know the will of God, Paul tells us what it is in Romans 12:1-2 (NIV) "Therefore, I urge you, brothers and sisters, in view of God's mercy, to offer your bodies as a living sacrifice, holy and pleasing to God—this is your true and proper worship. Do not conform to the pattern of this world, but be transformed by the renewing of your mind. Then you will be able to test and approve what God's will is—his good, pleasing and perfect will." Now when Paul says offer your body as a living sacrifice, it is not some sort of ritual that will involve your physical death. Jesus already paid that price, once and for all. Instead, it means to die to your selfish desires and submit yourself to God instead. If we truly do this we will be holy and pleasing to Him, which should be our goal. It means, once again that we turn from our sin and give Him all we are. This is the essence of real worship, submitting to God in every area of life, and anything less is, in fact, a form of idolatry.

Further Paul tells us not to conform to the pattern of the world. The reason for that is simple, the world is a mess. It runs under a different system, a system that has things upside down and backwards from the way it is supposed to be. Our world is currently, for the most part, completely opposite of the way God intended. This system was set in place by the one who came to steal, kill and destroy, the enemy of your soul, Satan himself. The effects of sin are running rampant everywhere, and they're trying to drag us into it's wake, but there is a better way. In order to get to that better way, we have to take on a radical non-conformity. We have to be different than the world. This way of thinking is really nothing new. Your mom probably showed it to you in not so many words when she said, "If all your friends were jumping off a bridge, would you do it, too?" The smart answer to that question is "No!" Instead you would go a different way, a way different from the pattern of this world.

Instead of conforming, and this is key, we are called to be transformed, by the renewing of our minds. We choose a new way of thinking, God's way. We look to the Word of God, prayer and the leading of the Holy Spirit to guide our steps and bring us to the righteous life God desires for us. When we submit out wills to His will, then and only then will we truly find Gods will, His good, pleasing and perfect will. It's when we find that will, and begin to live it out that we find life's true meaning. We come to understand that God is enough, that the price Jesus paid is enough, that His will is enough. His plan is enough and in Him, we will finally come to the place where we can say, "In Christ, I am enough!"

Epilogue
The World is Not Enough

I know that title sounds a little greedy, more like a quote from a James Bond villain, than a pastor, but please work with me, because this is really important. I originally thought about calling this chapter, "When You've Had Enough of the World," but I thought that might put forth the wrong message. Too many people get fed up with this world and decide to leave it on their own terms and that is always a tragic waste. Suicide is a permanent solution to a temporary problem and there is always a better way. If you're in despair, don't wait, get help right away, because hopefully through the course of this book you have seen, there is incredible reason for hope and at least part of that hope comes from you.

It's true. If you watch the news, it can be downright depressing. Each day it seems someone tries to invent a new way of doing harm to others. This should not be surprising. The apostle Paul, two thousand years ago, speaking of the sinfulness of humanity came right out and said, "...They invent ways of doing evil." (Romans 1:30 NIV) Our world is in a mess, but the good news is, this is not how it was intended to be. As such, the world is far from hopeless, as a matter of fact, there is great hope for our world and again, in Christ, you are part of that hope.

I know it's hard to believe. The problems look so big that it makes us feel incredibly small, but by now you should be recognizing the theme. In Christ you are enough. Maybe you can't fix the whole problem, but you can do something and the more people that do something, the better things get, but it goes deeper. Remember, God's plan is to redeem and restore. He wants to redeem creation, to return it to what it was created to be and to restore the relationship with humanity, broken by sin. At the end of the story, (which is not really the end at all) it will be as it was in the beginning. God living in perfect love with His creation for all eternity. This is what we're moving toward. This is the fulfillment of God's plan, and yes, we get to be a part of it.

Let's look at the words of Paul. In Romans 8:18 (NIV) Paul writes, "I consider that our present sufferings are not worth comparing with the glory that will be revealed in us." We can learn a few things from this verse. Let's get the bad news out of the way first. Suffering is inevitable. Life in this world will continue to be hard until creation is redeemed. The good news is the suffering is temporary. Remember what Jesus said? "I have told you these things, so that in me you may have peace. In this world you will have trouble." (John 16:33A NIV) I call this the promise of God that none of us want Him to keep. Nonetheless trouble is guaranteed in this broken world.

The Battle Rages

I really want to emphasize this point because so many people seem to think this is not the case and too often it is taught, or at least implied from our pulpits. People get the idea that coming to Christ is going to be the end of their troubles and when trouble comes to call, they get quickly disillusioned and upset with God. The reality in this broken world is we are in a battle. Author John Eldridge once said, "The story of your life is the story of the long and brutal assault on your heart by the one who knows what you could be and fears it." This is the essence of the battle we're in, in this world.

There is a villain in your story. He has been around since before time began. He started as an angel, but a greed for power made him desire to claim the throne of God. As a result, he was cast out of heaven and sentenced to destruction at the end of time. His name is Satan and his fate is already determined—eternal destruction. In this world, he has only one mission. To destroy that which God loves most, and what

God loves most is you. The battle around you is fierce, and the souls of humanity hang in the balance. Anything he can do to take you off mission and mess you up, he will do and that is why Jesus guarantees each of us trouble in this world—not easy street, not a free ride, but trouble. Some will try to tell you something else. Those people cannot be trusted. They are lying and if we believe those lies, we will become disillusioned at the first sign of trouble. Ironically Jesus told us about the trouble we can expect so that we can have peace in Him. He doesn't say He will spare us from trouble or pull us out of trouble. He tells us the trouble is coming so we are not shocked by it and He tells us about the trouble so we will be ready and know we are not alone. You see there is a second sentence in this verse and it says:

"But take heart! I have overcome the world."

This is the good news in a nutshell. It's not that we will be spared trouble, or pulled out of trouble, it's that He will be with us through the trouble and He has already won the victory. We may have trouble, but if you are a believer, the One who has overcome death and hell and the grave is on your side and by your side through it. You're still in the battle, but the One who has already won the battle is on your side. This is the truly great news because, as Scripture says, "the one who is in you is greater than the one who is in the world." (1 John 4:4 NIV)

This is why Paul can say that our current struggles cannot compare with the glory that will be revealed in us. Can it be that struggle reveals God's glory? Absolutely! The truth of the matter is we can best see the glory of God in the way He brings us through our struggles. If we don't go through the struggles, we may miss the glory. It's hard to see God's faithfulness if we never need Him to come through, but when He comes through, not only do we see His faithfulness but others can see it through us and when that happens, glory is revealed. The old saying is that your test becomes your testimony and it's absolutely true. The trials reveal the faithfulness of God.

In Romans 8:19 (NIV) we see it's a lot bigger than our struggles. "For the creation waits in eager expectation for the children of God to be revealed." To really get a handle on what this means, let's look at politics, specifically American politics. Don't worry, I'm going to stay neutral. If you watch the news, you'll see that at any given time, there are many people dissatisfied with our leadership, and Christians, even though we are commanded by God to pray for our leaders, are not immune from airing our complaints. One of the things we often end up lamenting is the fact that the morals of our nation do not line up with the teachings of scripture. We often place these problems firmly at the feet of our leaders, but is that correct? Let's dissect the situation.

If the leaders of the nation are the problem, and I'm not saying they're not a contributing factor, but the question is who picked them? We the people did. The majority of voters went to the polls and selected these people. Voting is our privilege and our right and we should exercise the privilege every single time the opportunity presents itself, but let me ask you a follow up question. If the majority of Americans select a certain leader, chances are awfully good that this majority elected someone who reflects their values, right? If this is the case, and it is, then the leader is a reflection of his or her constituents, or at least a reflection of the ones who voted for the leader. Perhaps I am slightly oversimplifying, but I think it's safe to assume that the leaders look like the majority of the voting population and the voting population, at least to some degree, resembles the leadership. To really oversimplify it, we pick who we are.

So the problem in a democracy is not the leaders, it's the people. To change the leaders, at least for the long haul, we need to change the population. If we want more moral leaders, for example, the population must become more moral and this is where we want to throw up our hands and say "That's impossible." No, it isn't. There is a group of people in our world that is tasked with changing the hearts of the population, or at least bringing the message that changes hearts. That group is called the Church of Jesus Christ. We are charged with taking the Gospel to the ends of the earth. It is the Gospel and it is Jesus Christ that changes hearts. If we want a better nation, the Gospel is the answer. We need to be a great commission church, taking the Gospel to our friends and our neighbors and to the community and the nation and to the ends of the earth. If we want to see things change, it starts with us. It starts, one heart, and one life at a time, because a heart submitted to Jesus is a changed heart, a changed heart is a changed life and enough changed lives will change a nation. This is what Paul is talking about when he said creation is waiting for the children of God to be revealed. Are you a child of God? Because if you are and you will submit yourself to the calling of your Lord and master, you are enough in Him to become part of the change you want to see.

Paul goes on in Romans 8:20-21 (NIV) to say, "For the creation was subjected to frustration, not by its own choice, but by the will of the one who subjected it, in hope that the creation itself will be liberated from its bondage to decay and brought into the freedom and glory of the children of God." What this means is the hard times and struggles we face in this broken down world are designed to bring about its redemption by motivating the children of God to leave the shackles of their sin behind and take up their crosses and the truth that sets men free. Our purpose in this world as believers is to do our part in bringing about the Kingdom of God, by spreading His Gospel, the good news of Jesus, until everyone has heard.

I've heard people lament, "How long will God let this go on?" I have heard other people who stopped believing that Jesus will ever return, or that He was ever really here in the first place, because of how long the world has been in this mess. That is a fallacy. Scripture tells us why God waits. 2 Peter 3:9 (NIV) gives us the answer to the conundrum. "The Lord is not slow in keeping his promise, as some understand slowness. Instead he is patient with you, not wanting anyone to perish, but everyone to come to repentance." The patient, loving God is waiting patiently until everyone bhas had the opportunity to receive eternal life through Jesus, because He desires to save us and to be in relationship with us forever. What is He waiting on? He's waiting on us? In Matthew 24:14 Jesus said, "And this gospel of the kingdom will be preached in the whole world as a testimony to all nations, and then the end will come." If we want to see this broken system, with all its hurt and pain to come to an end, the answer is simple, take the Gospel to the ends of the earth, until everyone has heard.

What comes next? The world becomes enough. Creation becomes all that it was intended to be, and it will stay that way forever. Revelation 21:3-5 breaks it down. "Look! God's dwelling place is now among the people, and he will dwell with them. They will be his people, and God himself will be with them and be their God. 'He will wipe every tear from their eyes. There will be no more death' or mourning or crying or pain, for the old order of things has passed away." He who was seated on the throne said, "I am making everything new!" Then he said, "Write this down, for these words are trustworthy and true."

The world is not enough, but one day it will be. The old order of things, the brokenness of this world will one day pass and be replaced with something new and beautiful and perfect and without the effects of sin to return us to the mess we're in, it will stay that way forever. A perfect world is coming and when it comes it will be more than enough. In the mean time, we who believe, work with our Lord to bring about His Kingdom. You are up to the task, because He put in you what you need to do your part, and anything you lack will help you to depend on Him. He has you covered. In other words, in Christ Jesus...

You are ENOUGH!

About the Author

Dave Weiss is an artist, a pastor and a person passionate about helping people to become everything that God has created them to be. He is pastor of Springfield Church of the Brethren in Coopersburg, PA. In addition, Dave is founder of AMOKArts, a creative arts/speaking ministry dedicated to helping the church to embrace it's God given creativity and to creatively empower people to take the unchanging message of the Gospel to an ever changing world.

When he's not pastoring and traveling, Dave enjoys writing and making art. You can read Dave's daily blog and find out more about his speaking ministry at AMOKArts.com.

Dave is married to Dawn. They have two adult sons and reside in Mohrsville, PA.

Is Your Congregation Enough?
If you've been blessed by what's in this book
consider bringing Dave in to your church
to share one of his creative ministry presentations.
Find out more at AMOKArts.com

Can't Get Enough?
Join the Enough community on Facebook at
facebook.com/enoughbook1/

Enough

Made in the USA
Middletown, DE
29 January 2018